The Warrior's Tools

The Warrior's Tools

Plains Indian Bows,
Arrows and Quivers

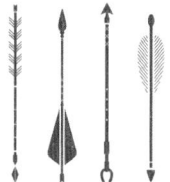

ERIC SMITH

THE ROADRUNNER PRESS
OKLAHOMA CITY, OKLAHOMA

Copyright © 2019 by Eric Smith
Cover Copyright © The RoadRunner Press
Cover Photo and Interior Illustrations © Eric Smith
Illustration of Arrows © Lera Efremova / Shutterstock.com
Cover Design: Jeanne Devlin
Longman, Green & Co. map: Chelmsford Historical Society

The RoadRunner Press is committed to publishing works of quality and integrity. The story, the experiences, and the words shared here are the author's alone.

All rights reserved.

The RoadRunner Press
Oklahoma City, Oklahoma
www.TheRoadRunnerPress.com

Bulk copies or group sales of this book available by contacting orders@theroadrunnerpress.com or calling (405) 524-6205.

FIRST EDITION MARCH 2019
Printed in the USA

Library of Congress Control Number: 2019934430

Publisher's Cataloging-In-Publication Data
(Prepared by The Donohue Group, Inc.)

Names: Smith, Eric (James Eric), 1975- author.
Title: The warrior's tools : Plains Indian bows, arrows and quivers / Eric Smith.
Description: First edition. | Oklahoma City, Oklahoma : The RoadRunner Press, 2019.
Identifiers: ISBN 9781937054830 (HC) | ISBN 9781937054892 (TP) | ISBN 9781937054908 (ebook)
Subjects: LCSH: Indian weapons--Great Plains. | Indians of North America--Implements. | Bow and arrow--Great Plains.
Classification: LCC E59.A68 S658 2019 (print) | LCC E59.A68 (ebook) | DDC 355.8241097078--dc23

10 9 8 7 6 5 4 3 2 1

*To the memory of Austin Dennis
of Pauls Valley, Oklahoma*

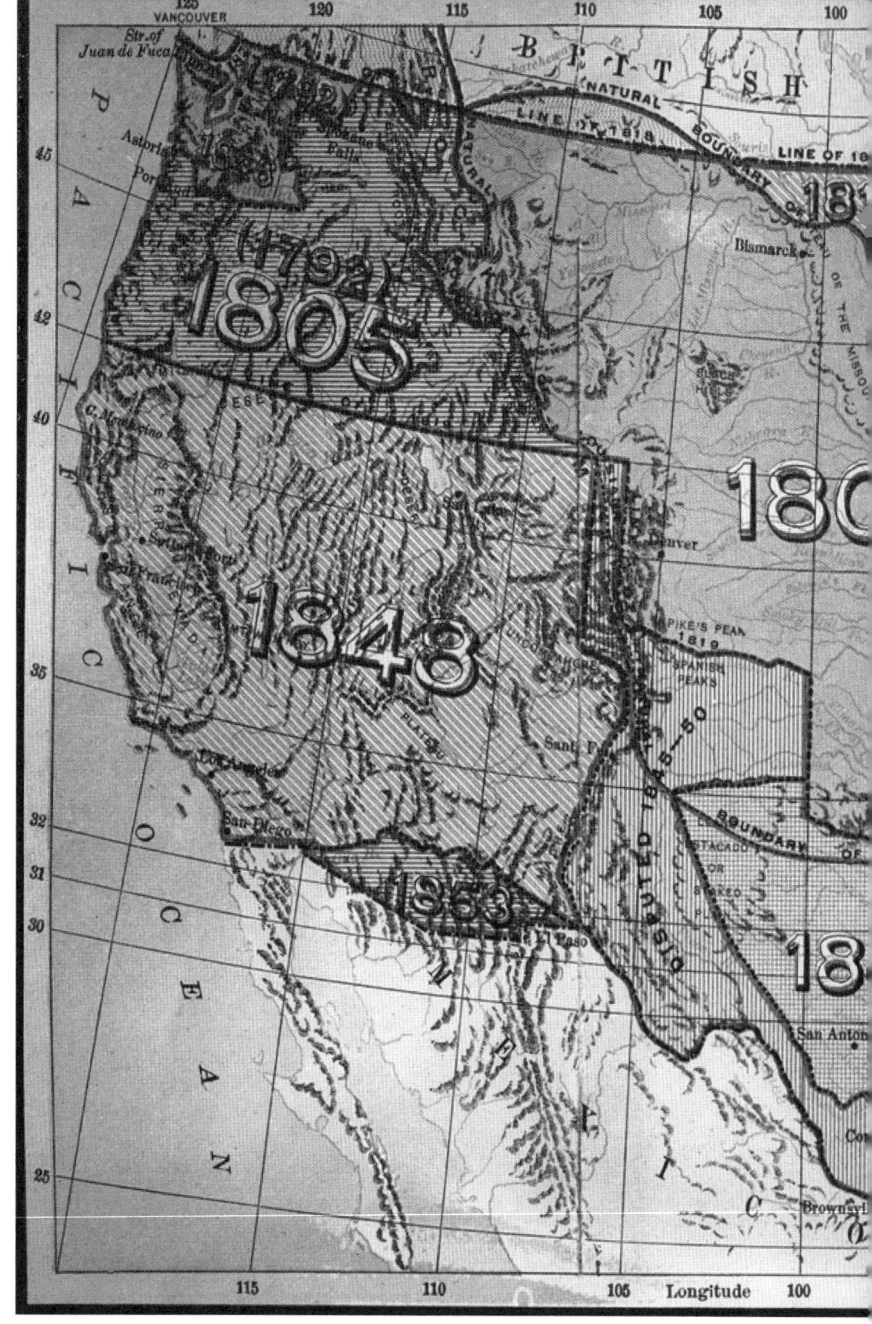

TERRITORIAL GROWTH
OF THE
UNITED STATES OF AMERICA
1783—1866.

Table of Contents

Foreword

Introduction

Chapter 1: *The Beginning* 1

Chapter 2: *Bow Designs* 7

Chapter 3: *Basic Bow Making* 19

Chapter 4: *Bending Bows to Shape* 35

Chapter 5: *All About Sinew* 39

Chapter 6: *Plains Indian Horn Bows, Part 1* 49

Chapter 7: *Plains Indian Horn Bows, Part 2* 65

Chapter 8: *Shooting the Short Bow* 77

Chapter 9: *Plains Indian Arrows* 87

Chapter 10: *Plains Indian Quivers* 101

Chapter 11: *Plains Indian Shields* 111

Chapter 12: *Final Thoughts* 121

Glossary and Diagrams 125

About the Author

Acknowledgments

Foreword

I was particularly honored when the author asked me to write the foreword for his new book, *The Warrior's Tools: Plains Indian Bows, Arrows, and Quivers*. Although we have known each other for a relatively short time, we have much in common. Not only do we share a similar ancestry as citizens of the Chickasaw Nation, but we also grew up in similar circumstances near the Washita River in southern Oklahoma.

Eric Smith's family was concentrated in and around the fertile farmlands of Pauls Valley, whereas my family had long been located farther south in the timbered hill country near the confluence of the Washita and Red Rivers close to the Texas border. Both of our Chickasaw families were historically influenced by adventurous Texans from south of the Red River as well.

Long before I came in contact with the author and learned of his passion for Native archery, I was friends with his grandfather Austin Dennis. We both were members of the Oklahoma Anthropological Society and were striving to explore, understand, and preserve the history and prehistory of our respective regions of the

Eric Smith

state. There were occasional interactions between us during annual meetings of the OAS members, normally held at the University of Oklahoma or at some of the spring or fall digs conducted by the society at various archaeological sites.

No stranger to hard work, Austin maintained a farm along Rush Creek just outside Pauls Valley, where he produced some of the largest, juiciest tomatoes and assorted other vegetables. In his spare time, he roamed across the valley functioning as an avocational archaeologist. From that vantage point, he could closely monitor some of the important archaeological sites in his vicinity. He was often instrumental in saving such sites from destruction or at least providing critical data to other professionals working out of the state archaeologist's office.

Over time, Austin also provided significant support to several students working on their graduate degrees involving the Arthur Site and other Plains village sites that were being threatened by construction.

During my professional career as a historian and archaeologist, Eric's grandfather would sometimes visit me at the Museum of the Great Plains in Lawton and the Fort Sill National Historic Landmark and Museum in Fort Sill, just north of Lawton, and we would talk shop about Oklahoma history or prehistory. I was always impressed by his friendliness as well as his intense curiosity and working knowledge on those subjects. He was a key player in producing special exhibits on local prehistory for the Washita River Valley Museum when it was established in his community.

Austin Dennis was nominated for the prestigious Golden Trowel Award by the OAS in recognition of his many outstanding achievements in support of the society. However, the competition was so strong that he received an alternative award of a special plaque with a seven-inch stone projectile point made of Florence chert mounted on it. He was so proud of this award that later, in accordance with old traditions, the plaque and projectile point were interred with him after he passed away.

It is obvious that this family history had a significant influence on Eric Smith in providing the foundation for his book with regards to the production and use of traditional Native archery equipment. Undoubtedly, he was also influenced in his undertaking through immersion with his wife's family heritage from the Numunu, or Comanche people. The Chickasaw and Comanche cultures have strong histories of warrior traditions, with each having the tribal motto of "Unconquered" or "Unconquerable." It was in this context of working with the Southern Plains tribes that I first became aware of his reputation as an exceptional Native bowyer and craftsman.

It is equally clear that the author has succeeded in packaging within the covers of this book the benefit of thirty years' experience working with master tribal bowyers, conducting historical research, and hands-on trial-and-error experimentation to understand the nature of specific construction techniques. The scope of the book not only covers the production of bows, arrows, quivers, and shields but also delves into the cultural and physical nature of the basic raw materials used in their production. In so doing, Smith also attempts to develop a better understanding of what worked, and what did not work, from both a contemporary and historical perspective.

The text is written in simple language designed to enhance the reader's understanding of materials and techniques that could otherwise be difficult to discuss within another context. For example, the subject of assembling a horn-reinforced bow is scarce in other historical references and not easy to understand even when museum specimens are available for examination. Only after the direct trial-and-error experimentation by an experienced bowyer could the success or failure of the materials and techniques be legitimately determined. Field testing of those experimental specimens is the ultimate indicator of success or failure, and the author provides ample data resulting from his experience.

Of particular interest in this work are the correlations between using the appropriate materials and production techniques in manufacturing bows and arrows and the historical use of the weapons themselves. Regional variations of materials and processes are discussed that might have been determined by available resources and cultural perspectives.

Frequent mention in the text of bois d'arc, or Osage orange, wood as a preferred material for bow making in the Southern Plains reminded this writer of an incident in the mid-1850s when the Cheyennes from the Northern Plains, during a lull in tribal conflict, undertook a long journey to the south in search of horses, captives, and *yellow bows*. They had determined those resources were either limited (horses and captives) or absent (yellow bows) in the north but were readily available to the Comanches and the Kiowas in the south.

The *yellow bows* on the battlefields indicated that the weapons were newly made from the bois d'arc trees that grew along the Red River valley between Oklahoma and Texas, but not encountered farther north during that period. Normally, the yellow wood turns a rich brown in color with the passage of time, but the newly made yellow bows stood out on the battlefields after encounters with the Comanche or Kiowa warriors. Comanche and Kiowa parties they met along the way, however, were not helpful in identifying sources or providing directions to the Cheyenne.

Although the Cheyenne's journey did ultimately extend into the interior of Mexico and a small quantity of horses and materials for yellow bows was secured while passing through the Red River country, the trip was considered a failure because of hostilities along the way with Mexican vaqueros, Texans, and other forces.

The Warrior's Tools

A unique incident involving the production and use of traditional archery equipment that is noteworthy in the context of this book occurred shortly after the conclusion of the Red River War, or Buffalo War, in the Southern Plains. With the final surrenders of the Comanches, Kiowas, Plains Apache, and other tribes at Fort Sill, Indian Territory (Oklahoma), in the spring of 1875, it was determined that selected individuals from those tribes would be confined as prisoners in Fort Marion, Florida. This separation from their people and their homeland was considered appropriate punishment for the more volatile or hostile individuals.

Some very unique and little known history occurred during that two-year period of confinement so far from home along the Florida seacoast. The buffalo-hunting warriors of the Plains became involved in some rather unusual activities such as shark hunting, production of pictographic art portfolios for tourists, and public archery. Arriving as prisoners and without weapons, they had to produce new bows and arrows to hold competitions and demonstrations for the public.

Archery at that time was experiencing a revival of interest and becoming a major recreational pastime for the genteel ladies of the eastern seaboard. Commercial advertising of various products often portrayed Victorian ladies wearing long dresses and big hats while aiming a longbow and arrow toward a specific target of economic opportunity. It naturally followed that those Victorian tourists wanted to experience archery with the "wild Indians" of the American West. Some of the artwork produced by the warriors depicted themselves with bows and arrows giving archery lessons to the visitors.

A true paradox in history!

—Towana Spivey
Curator, historian, and archaeologist

Introduction

The written record on Great Plains self bows is sparse at best. Despite the paucity of a written record, Eric Smith has been able to replicate ancient self bows that are both authentic and functional. Little wonder that his dedication to the bowyer craft and his focus on the Great Plains self bow are recognized on local, regional, and global scales. Thus, Smith is well suited for the writing of this book, which will enlighten his readers on the little known history of the Plains self bow and may well inspire them to pick up a piece of Osage orange or hickory and shape it into a bow.

Smith's audience will appreciate his comprehensive approach to making the Great Plains self bow and associated equipment (arrows, quivers, and shields), which emanates from countless hours visiting with tribal elders (especially his adopted Comanche people), exploring archival documents, and experimenting with various materials and methods.

His vast knowledge of the history and niche as well as the ability to accurately reconstruct authentic Plains self bows, arrows, and quivers make his work second to none. Smith has built more

Eric Smith

than one thousand bows in over a quarter-century. His bows are on display in private homes, museums, and art galleries in more than twenty-five countries. Although Smith's bows adorn the walls of great museums and art galleries, most could also be used to harvest bison, elk, and white-tailed deer.

The first chapter of the book *The Warrior's Tools: Plains Indian Bows, Arrows, and Quivers* is systematically organized and provides the history of bows and bow making, types of bows, and materials used to make bows. The succeeding chapters strike a nice balance between Smith's passion for bow making, cultural qualities of the bow, and historical perspective of bows used by the Great Plains Indians over the past two hundred years while explaining how to make self bows, arrows, and quivers.

The content of each chapter could be processed independently by the reader; thus, an individual interested in making an arrow could read Chapter 9 and make an authentic arrow. Smith draws his audience into his work, with stories he has read in books or learned firsthand from tribal elders.

It is obvious that Smith has a spiritual connection with his work, which he also shares with his readers. He defines terms used in bow making, explains which trees make the best bows and arrows, how to select the best wood (and botanically which part of the tree's anatomy is best suited for a bow or arrow), how to cure the wood, and how to shape the wood into a bow. Smith also provides excellent details on bow styles (horn bows, antler bows, deflexed, reflexed), nock placement, stringing the bow, decorating the bow, and making associated equipment such as arrows and quivers. In addition, he introduces tools used in the past and present by bowyers as well as how to properly use each tool.

Smith's work is the first comprehensive written record documenting two hundred years of history and the making of the bows used by the Great Plains tribes. He continues to strengthen his

The Warrior's Tools

knowledge of the bowyer craft through reading books, researching tribal archives, and listening to tribal elders. Through experimenting with old and new designs in bows and associated equipment, Smith continues to broaden his understanding of the many bow styles and bow-making techniques used by the Great Plains tribes.

Smith is a well recognized master bowyer. As a hunter of big game animals who uses bow and arrow, admires Native American history and culture, and has little time to read for pleasure, I find Smith's book to be refreshing, inspiring, and bursting with facts about the first people who inhabited the Great Plains of North America. Like the lyrics of a good song, the words from Eric Smith's book will continue to play in the minds of those who read it well after the book has been shelved.

Excellent work, my friend.

—**Kent Smith, Ph.D.**
Associate Dean, Office for the Advancement of American Indians in Medicine and Science;
Professor of Anatomy, Department of Anatomy and Cell Biology, Oklahoma State University Center for Health Sciences

Vertebrate Paleontology Research Associate, Sam Noble Oklahoma Museum of Natural History

Chapter 1
The Beginning

MY THIRTY-YEAR JOURNEY of making Plains Indian bows and arrows started in 1982. I was six years old and already my grandfather's shadow.

Paopa was an amateur archaeologist well respected in the archaeology community. He gave talks at the University of Oklahoma in Norman, helped students on digs, and worked for *National Geographic* one summer on a dig in our native Oklahoma. My grandfather's knowledge of the prehistoric people, flora, and fauna of this area was unrivaled.

As a boy, one of my favorite pastimes was to hunt arrowheads and talk about Native American culture with my grandfather. Our talks sometimes went on for hours, with me trying my best to soak up every word he had to share.

Hunting and fishing were a big part of our lives as well and therefore much time was spent practicing with bows and arrows. In my memories of childhood, I always seemed to have a bow with me. My uncles kept me in arrows, although I rarely had two alike. My uncles' patience—and their willingness to include me in their pastime—helped make possible the skills I have developed since. Along the way, I learned to keep my eyes and ears open, absorbing the secrets of the place we called home.

One ordinary summer day that year, I followed Paopa to the toolshed as I had so many times before. He handed me a hatchet and then took a bow saw off the shelf. He led me to the creek behind his house, pointing out various trees, naming each one, and explaining what to look for to distinguish one from another. Eventually, he pointed to a pecan tree and then to some pecans rotting on the ground.

"I know pecans well, Paopa," I said.

He said nothing but continued to walk. A little farther on, he pointed to a black walnut tree. He began to speak, but I interrupted before he could.

"I know about the black walnut tree, Paopa."

That time, he asked, "How do you know about pecan and black walnut trees?"

I answered him without a second's hesitation. "Uncle Tim and Uncle Gary chase me around the house throwing them at me—that's how!"

Paopa said not a word in response, but I can still recall the scowl that crossed his face. In silence, we continued to walk up the creek until we came across a cluster of bois d'arc trees, more commonly known as Osage orange or hedge apple.

That time, I remained quiet as Paopa explained that the wood of the Osage orange is the prized bowwood of many Indian tribes. He pointed out the patterns found in the bark, patterns that give a clue to what the underlying wood would look like. He had me join him in a search for a nice, straight limb with few knots. When Paopa finally found what he was looking for, a branch three inches around, he used the hatchet to remove the sharp thorns protruding from the bark.

Then he took the saw, cut the branch to about four feet in length, and handed it to me. I will never forget how heavy that limb was or how the white sap that oozed from the freshly cut end stuck to my hands and shirt. I dragged the branch all the way back to the house, anticipating the project to come.

Upon our return, we headed straight for the shed. Paopa put the tools back in their places, and then he picked up a wax candle, lit a small blowtorch, and melted the wax to cover each raw end of the limb. With the ends of the branch sealed, he hung the limb in the rafters of the old shed, explaining that the wood needed to sit for a while and dry.

It was beginning to look as if there would be no project on that day, but before my spirits could fall, Paopa reached behind the shed door, pulled out a similar length of wood, and said, "This one is ready."

My eyes must have lit up because he chuckled as he picked up a butcher knife, and we headed to the back porch. I recall some discussion about what the next step would be, if memory serves, but all I remember for sure is the thrill of knowing I was going to get to use that butcher knife on that Osage orange limb. At six years of age, things rarely get more exciting than that—unless maybe you're fleeing two uncles pelting you with walnuts and pecans.

Three years later, at the ripe old age of nine, I made my first Osage orange self bow using nothing more than a drawknife (a woodworker's blade with a handle at each end using for shaving wood), a wood rasp (a coarse file used to shape wood), and a butcher knife.

That bow was made from a branch very similar in width and length to that original Osage orange limb. With a squared design throughout, my little bow showed the limb's pith ring (the circular rings you see on a cross section of a limb or tree trunk) and had a bowstring made of baling twine. Making it gave me much enjoyment, and it was not long until I started another.

The bow-making bug had bitten me.

As the years progressed, I honed my skills in making bows (a trimmed rod of wood to which the bowstring is attached), working with various woods, and learning how to steam bows into various shapes. My grandfather poured all his knowledge of bows into me as well, and I never got my fill.

As my desire to build bows of various forms and from other materials grew, I became interested in sinew-backed bows and bows made from horn and antler. Paopa had taught me early on how to harvest deer tendon, or sinew, and to make hide glue, but making sinew-backed bows was out of the realm of his knowledge, so I was on my own this time.

I read everything I could find on the subject and looked for bowyers who might help me. I was hindered at the time by such bow makers being few and far between. The Internet had yet to be invented; information did not flow among tribes and countries like it does today. The collection at our local public library contained only generalized books on Native Americans with little cross-referencing on bow making other than the occasional notation or random passage.

So I did what any curious fellow with a passion would do: I began to experiment on my own with sinew and how to apply it to my bows. It took some time, but I figured out how to sinew-back a bow. That was an important step in the direction I wanted to take as a bowyer. Other projects of more complicated design were soon under way.

I eventually began to experiment with sheep horn—and ruined three nice sets of horns in the process. However, my first attempt at making a bow from a set of elk antlers was successful, although I do believe that without my knowledge of bow making and sinew-backing bows, I would have failed at that one as well.

Practice makes for good experience, I found, and you should know that I failed many times along the way. I learned not to let the failures stop me, and the successes I did have kept the fire burning.

At the time of this writing, I have made more than seven hundred self bows (a simple bow made from a single piece of wood) and a little more than three hundred composite bows (a traditional bow made from horn, wood, and sinew laminated together). Somewhere along the way, I quit keeping an exact count.

For many years, I made my living as a full-time bowyer, sending bows to more than twenty-five countries around the world. More recently, my bow making has led to other experiences, including the U.S. Department of the Interior's Bureau of Indian Education hiring me to teach Native American high school students archery history and how to make bows and arrows. To my knowledge, it is the first class of its kind to be offered at a Native American boarding school. I have also taught bow making to youngsters from reservations throughout the United States. I have made bows for Hollywood productions, including twenty-seven sinew-backed bows, ten self bows, and more than 260 arrows for the 2015 Academy Award winning movie *The Revenant*, which starred Leonardo DiCaprio and Tom Hardy.

Having my work recognized is satisfying, but I care more about preserving the art of making bows, arrows, quivers, and shields. And that can't happen if people don't have a way to learn the craft. Not everyone grows up with a grandfather with Paopa's knowledge. And that is why I have written this book.

Many fine books on making bows and arrows now exist—there are even YouTube videos on how to make or string a bow—but some are so technical that the average person can easily get lost. I wanted to do a book that everyone could understand.

Eric Smith

I have tried to focus on the heart of the subject so you can get into the workshop sooner rather than later. Think of this book as a launchpad—and realize that you can read all the books in the world on making bows and arrows, but you will learn more about both in a day's time by trying to make either than you can in a week's worth of reading about them.

Chapter 2
Bow Designs

THE PLAINS INDIAN TRIBE lived on the greater Interior Plains of North America, including the Great Plains of North America and the prairies of Canada. Their bows had similarities, but designs among the Plains tribes varied greatly. What the bows shared was a general length of three to four feet. The longest Plains bow I have ever seen was a rare fifty-two inches in length.

The D-shaped self bow, which looks like the capital letter "D" from the side when braced, was a common sight on the Plains—used by the Comanches in the south and the Sioux in the north. And then there was the picturesque and powerful five-curve bow seen in so many Western paintings—a bow with limbs that curve away from the archer and are reflexed at the handle, deflexed at the midlimb, and recurved at the tips.

Other bow designs existed, but before one can compare bows, it is important to know the materials used by bowyers because the materials often dictate what bow can be produced.

One of the most common bowwoods used on the Plains was the Osage orange, or bois d'arc, which had captured my imagination as a boy. Bois d'arc literally means "bow wood" in American French, but through the years, that was boiled down to *bodark*.

Other woods that work well for a bow include hickory, mulberry, hackberry, and ash, to name a few. Many other usable woods exist, but the above will work for our needs here.

Some of those favored woods did not grow on the Northern Plains; the Osage orange is plentiful primarily in a small area centered in the Red River Valley in what is now southern Oklahoma and northern Texas; although, it can be found throughout Oklahoma now. Yet many Osage orange bows have been collected from northern tribes, most likely a result of bows being taken as plunder in raids or battle. It seems quite plausible that a warrior coming across an enemy bow left on the battlefield and finding it to be a good weapon, wouldn't leave it behind.

Another way to acquire Osage orange bows, however, was through trade. Throughout history, tribes who were mortal enemies have been known to make truces to trade for a few days before returning to war. If you traded with a neighboring tribe and that tribe traded with a neighboring tribe, before long, things made their way around. That held true with bows and bowwood as well as other goods. Trade routes were far more extensive than most people today realize.

The same held true for tribes going off to war.

I have read of Plains warriors who were gone from home so long on a war trail that when they finally returned, their wives had remarried, their kids had grown a head taller, and they had long been declared dead. Needless to say, it was quite possible for someone to use a bow made from wood that did not grow within a thousand miles. Thus, was the vast trade system on the historic Great Plains.

Bow lengths among the Comanches and Kiowa of the Southern Plains averaged forty-plus inches, and most bows were of the D-shaped bow design. Sinew-backed bows from this area existed, but they were not the norm.

I had the privilege of knowing the last true Comanche bow maker, Carney Saupitty Sr. of Apache, Oklahoma. He was not only a tribal historian, fluent first speaker, and singer of songs but also a master bowyer. On many an occasion over a cup of coffee, we discussed the ins and outs of Southern Plains archery. Saupitty was familiar with the sinew-backed bow and its construction, but he told me the Comanches in general did not sinew-back their bows. It was unnecessary because of the quality of the bois d'arc wood available in the area.

Bodark wood is often considered the best or second-best bow-wood in the world. It takes a back seat only to yew wood, which, although found on the West Coast of the United States up into Alaska, is more common to Asia and Europe.

Many Southern Plains bows are distinguished by a squared design one-inch- to one-and-a-half inches wide, sometimes tapering at the tips. Some of the bows will have a mild setback in the handle and a slight deflex in the tips, making a slight reflex-deflex design.

The frequency of the appearance of deflexing is debatable, because any bowyer knows deflexing the tips of a bow takes away from its cast, or the distance it can shoot an arrow. So the presence of permanent deflexing could stem from extensive use of the bow or from years of leaving the bow strung rather than from the original design of the bow maker. Deflexing might also be from the bow's having been used before the wood was seasoned. Short bows do have a tendency to take some set when used a lot.

Southern Plains bows had double nocks at the top and bottom, single nocks at the top and the bottom on opposite sides, or single at the top and double at the bottom. There was no standard, it seems. You see this same nock conformation all over the Plains; however, sometimes the way the tips were shaped provides a clue to the tribal origin of the bow.

The majority of the bows I have looked at from the Southern Plains use Osage orange wood, but I have seen several made from hackberry or mulberry. Sometimes it can be difficult to identify the wood of an old bow unless it is Osage orange, the latter being unmistakable because of its color. When freshly cut, bodark wood is a brilliant yellow, and it ages to a deep, dark reddish brown. No other wood on the Plains looks the same.

I have found sinew to be the bowstring of choice among most Plains tribes with a low brace height, usually about four inches. In many bows, you see a protrusion at the upper tip where some kind of decoration was once attached, say horsehair or a piece of human scalp. Such protrusions appear on sinew bows throughout the Plains. None of the bows I have studied from the Southern Plains have a handle section wrapped with buckskin or cloth. They are all plain.

As you move northward, bow design changes somewhat, as do the woods from which the bows are crafted. Ash and hickory come into play—as well as woods obtained in trade from east and west of the Sioux lands, not to mention those obtained in trade from the Cheyennes to the south, who often visited their northern cousins.

I have found that Sioux bows varied more within the tribe than in any other Plains tribe. The Sioux made bows with unmistakable handle sections, narrowing the handle to wider flared limbs, then a sharp narrowing of the last four inches or so at the bow tips. They made deep-set back handles in some bows, giving the bow a "B" shape when strung.

The Sioux also made simple D-shaped bows, as seen on the Southern Plains. They made sheep-horn composite bows and even bows with great reflex added, possibly because a bow that is reflexed will have improved cast and speed versus a bow that is straight limbed or deflexed.

The Sioux made and used a plethora of bows, and throughout the tribe's history, did it with great success.

All such bows can be made with or without sinew backing. Bows from hickory and ash benefit from adding sinew because hickory is prone to taking set, whereas ash is known to explode without warning. Sinewing improves a bow's performance and adds a safety factor, but many bows from those woods were not sinew-backed. By all accounts, I am sure they served their masters well. All I am saying is that those particular woods benefit from the addition of sinew.

On the Central and Northern Plains, you see more bows with sinew backing than you do in the South. We have already established that the bowwood on the Southern Plains was particularly resilient. What makes a bowwood resilient is its qualities of tension (the elongating force that runs along the back of the bow when it is braced or drawn) and compression (the force that attempts to shorten). When you have a wood that is good in compression and weak in tension, you need sinew backing to add the needed tension for a workable bow.

Ideally, you also need a wood that has both of those qualities to make a lasting bow. When you add sinew to any bow that has both qualities, you can draw the bow farther than you could without the sinew. This adds more tension to the bow itself, therefore improving cast and speed.

If properly tillered and made from good bowwood, a bow that bends through the handle should draw half of its overall length. Bending through the handle means the whole bow is acting as one working limb. In other words, the bow bends throughout its entire length to achieve full draw. A bow of forty-eight inches in total length of this design with a spot-on tiller should draw twenty-four inches. That would make the picture of the bow, when in full draw, look C-shaped.

If you have a bow that is forty-eight inches long and the handle section is stiff in a five-inch section and does not bend, you have an upper working limb and a lower working limb. These two limbs have to be tillered the same and work as one to make the bow shoot properly. That stiff handle section of five inches leaves you with only forty-three inches of working limb. It will reduce your maximum draw length to twenty-one-and-a-half inches unless sinew is added, which will add another inch or two of draw length.

The short bows used by the Plains tribes on horseback came late in the history of the tribes. They were often referred to as horse or pony bows, but I use the term short bows to describe them.

Despite conventional wisdom, the horseback culture of the Plains tribes, romanticized in so many books and movies, covered only a brief period in history. The Comanches were the first to be fully mounted and on their way to a nomadic lifestyle by about 1730. From then on, the horse began to be used by many of the Plains tribes, eventually reaching the Sioux in about 1760 to 1770. I consider the last great battle of the Plains Indian horseback culture to be the two-day Battle of the Greasy Grass, most commonly referred to as Custer's Last Stand, in late June 1876. After that, few mounted warriors rode across the Plains in any great number, and the horseback culture of the Plains tribes faded into memory.

While it flourished, however, bows became shorter and shorter, a product of necessity. A short bow, although much tougher to master, was much easier to use while on horseback, and hunters and warriors quickly saw the benefits of that.

When riding within a few yards of your prey—either a buffalo or another person—accuracy was increased because of your being close to the target. That is not to say that short bows would not do damage at greater distances, but much practice was needed to master such a skill. No wonder some of the first things made for a young Indian boy were a bow and a few blunt arrows. From the time boys could walk, most practiced shooting continually.

The Plains tribes were split in two groups: Tribes that were fully nomadic in the eighteenth and nineteenth centuries, such as the Arapaho, Assiniboin, Blackfoot, Cheyenne, Comanche, Crow, Gros Ventre, Kiowa, Lakota, Lipan, Plains Apache (or Apache Tribe of Oklahoma, as they are called now), Plains Cree, Plains Ojibwe, Sarsi, Nakoda, and Tonkawa. The other tribes were semi-sedentary, living in villages and raising a variety of crops but also still hunting buffalo. Those included the Arikara, Hidatsa, Iowa, Kaw, Kitsai, Mandan, Missouria, Omaha, Osage, Otoe, Pawnee, Ponca, Quapaw, Wichita, Santee Dakota, Yanktonai, and Yankton Dakota.

Both types of tribes used bows that were within a standard of usability on horseback and of lengths generally shorter than fifty-two inches. It seems certain that those same tribes used longer bows when hunting on foot. When the horse came to the tribes, however, hunting changed, making it easier to hunt buffalo, although deer, antelope, and elk were also still hunted in great numbers. I have always believed that many of those tribes made and still used long bows well into the horseback culture; they just did not use the long bow on horseback.

People of the past were as individualistic and with personal preferences as we are today. Decoration is seen on many bows and it is not there just for looks. It usually held deep meaning. Most symbols depicted a battle exploit, a good luck charm, or a talisman. Paint color was chosen for the protecting properties associated with it by the bow owner.

Unless you were the owner of the bow, however, it is hard to say for sure what the decorations on any particular bow mean, but one can imagine. Horse tracks might represent a horse stolen or an enemy shot from horseback. A human scalp tassel hanging from the bow could represent an enemy killed. Bear fur tied to the bow might represent the power or spirit of a mighty animal. But we cannot know for sure.

As we begin to discuss bow design, we need to keep in mind that during this period of history, many tribes had metalware—knives, files, hammers, and a variety of other tools, most obtained by trading furs and robes with fur traders and mountain men but others collected on raids and travels. The Comanches were making raids into Mexico and stealing metal for arrowpoints and knives so long ago that they do not recall a time in their own history when they did not have iron arrowheads. As a result, making a bow in that period of time was not as hard as it would have been when the tribe had access only to flint and stone.

The D-shaped bow was a common design that when unstrung or unbraced stood virtually straight. The bow could be left stiff in the handle if desired, but that would not impact the looks of the bow when braced. Your overall shape would look like the letter "D" when strung, and it would look somewhat like the letter "C" when drawn, with a little less curl at the ends. That bow design could be found all over the Plains.

The five-curve bow of the Plains, or the Cupid's bow, as it is often called, was usually sinew-backed and had a handle that was set back toward the shooter in a reflex. The limbs were sometimes deflexed, and the ends of the bow were recurved. The five curves were accounted for in the handle, each limb, and each tip, consisting of five curves along the length of the bow. In some bows, the limbs were not deflexed but took that shape when strung, giving the bow the shape of the letter "B" when braced with recurves on the end. The recurve seen on the ends of Plains bows were not of the curvature we see today but rather shallow in comparison.

Because the handle does not bend and is stiff, a bow of this design usually kicks in the handle or vibrates in the handle. It seems to be the heaviest part of the bow, and the limb vibration resonates to the handle. The stiff handle shortens draw length. Therefore, the sinew-backing on a bow of this design can be helpful in getting a few extra inches of draw and thus more power. The design was seen in most of the Plains but was used more in the central and northern Plains.

The reflexed bow is a bow that is similar to the D-shaped bow when unstrung, but the bow has a reflex throughout its entire length, giving it a reverse "C" shape when unbraced. This can be a small amount of reflex, an extreme amount of reflex, or anywhere in between. This bow works well with a sinew backing, which adds even more cast and speed to the design.

The reflexed bow usually looks like the D-shaped bow when braced, but it will outperform most bows of similar length and draw weight. That can be credited to its limbs holding reflex, which adds great amounts of energy to the bow. In my opinion, this design is superior to the others.

It can be argued that recurved tips achieve the same result. That is true, but an overall reflex throughout a bow will add more speed and cast to the bow's performance than recurved tips alone. If you add recurved tips to a reflexed bow that has no deflex, you have an effective combination.

Some reflexed bows were made with a stiff handle, giving a shallow gull-wing shape when strung, although not as extreme as in the five-curve bows. That design was another seen throughout the Plains.

The reflexed-deflexed bow is similar to the five-curve bow, but the tips are not recurved. In most cases, the bow has a stiff handle set back toward the shooter in a reflex, and the limbs are deflexed. That bow has a "B" shape when braced. Bows of this design are often sinew-backed, but it is not necessary. Bows of this design are seen throughout the Plains too.

The last bow design to discuss is a pitiful one to say the very least, and that is the deflexed bow, a bow design that lacks both beauty and function. In fact, I find it to be one of the worst designs used among the Plains tribes, and I will never understand why it is seen so often.

Basically, a deflexed bow has limbs that have been deflexed toward the shooter, although it is possible that the bow was at one time a D-shaped bow that set after much use or perhaps was originally made from staves that were not quite cured and so took on an extreme set over time. As we discussed before, D-shaped bows do take on a little set over time, but I have seen bows that had what I am sure was purposely put deflex in the limbs.

The only redeeming factor for doing that, in my opinion, is that when the bow is braced, there is not as much tension on the string. Early draw weight on a bow of this design would be low, but I remain certain that it would gain poundage, or stack, as it is called, quickly when coming to the last few inches of draw. I have made a few bows of this design to see if I was missing any particular good quality or overlooking anything in the details. I have yet to discover the benefits of the design.

When it comes to shaping bows into different designs, that is done using dry heat or steam or bending a roughed-out piece of green wood into shape and then allowing it to dry while being held in position.

Many Indian bowyers incorporate the use of natural animal grease to achieve the bends they desire for their bows. That might also be how it was done in the past. Tribes on the Plains acquired pots for cooking, and those pots could have been used for steaming wood into shape for bows. However, I believe dry heating and heat and grease were the more common methods at the time.

The Warrior's Tools

For one, a bow greased to obtain a shape would be sinew-backed, and then the wood would have to be degreased. That could be done by rinsing the stave with water and ash. Plant ash is a known degreaser, and the tribes had easy access to fire ash.

Other bow designs were used among the Plains tribes, but I have found the above designs to be the mainstays of the horseback culture.

Chapter 3
Basic Bow Making

THE PLAINS INDIANS traded for tools and used many of the same tools we use today to make their bows. Drawknives and files were obtained through trade. With the arrival of those tools, bow making became much easier for the bowyer, who previously had had to use stone, flint, and lots of muscle to work suitable pieces of wood into bows.

It was said that a good bow was worth a horse in trade back then. So even all those years ago, the bow held high value. A man who could make them was more than likely better off than most—and respected among his tribesmen.

I do not think every tribal member could make bows and arrows, but I do believe all tribesmen shared an appreciation for the warrior's tools and an understanding of the way they were created. Just as there are specialists in every field, the Plains Indians had master bowyers, arrow makers, string builders, and point makers. You might own a bow made by one man and arrows made by still another and so on. When men reached the age at which they no longer went to war and were too old to hunt, they still had to survive. I believe many of those older warriors probably made weapons for the younger men and received meat, robes, horses, and other needed items for their services.

Being a learned skill, bow making was usually passed down from older generations to the young just as many skilled trades still are today. Women would also pass down to their daughters and granddaughters how to make lodges and tan robes. The men would do the same with how to make hunting tools and weapons. Together, they ensured that each new generation had the skills necessary for the tribe to survive.

I could devote volumes to the making of bows and the many kinds of bows. Instead, I am going to explain how to make one bow, a basic self bow, in a manner easy to understand. These steps are the same methods and tools used by the Plains Indian bowyers of old.

1. Learn the vocabulary

Before we start, let me suggest that you go to the glossary in the back of this book and review some of the basic bow-making vocabulary we will be using in the chapters to come. I am sure the Plains Indians had terminology equal to the bow-making terms we use now, but I have never seen any such list in written form. More likely than not, it has been lost to history. So we will work from this list.

2. Understand the material

In teaching high school students, I knew I had to keep things simple and straightforward. I made time for them to hack away at pieces of wood just to get the feel of what they were supposed to do. We also went over basic bow-making terminology and safety instructions beforehand. Once every student could tell me what all the commonly used terms meant, I let them have at it.

I liked to describe the parts of wood to them by using a telephone book and a block of bodark as visual aids. The phone book represented the piece of wood. Its cover was the bark, which I would then point out on the bodark.

As I ripped the cover off the phone book, I explained that this was the equivalent to removing the bark on a bowstave. With the cover gone, the white pages were the first pages to be exposed. I explained that those first pages represented the sapwood, or white wood, on the bowstave, and then I pointed out the layer of sapwood, or white wood, on the actual woodblock.

Next, I would tear out the white pages until I reached the first yellow page. I told the students the yellow pages represented the layers of hardwood, or heartwood, of the bowstave, and again, I pointed to the corresponding part of the bodark. I explained that we had to get to the hardwood—by peeling away the layers of bark and then sapwood—before we could start to rough out the bow.

Reaching the hardwood layer led to the next challenge: The hardwood has to form one single layer across the entire back of the bow. To make that clear, I ripped several of the yellow pages diagonally, explaining that if you cut through the layers of hardwood in that manner, you would have what is called a growth-ring violation. That violation would cause the layers of the wood to lift up when the bow is braced or drawn and will result in a failure.

The phone-book analogy seemed to explain the process of getting a bowstave down to the growth ring—at least none of the students ever raised a hand with any questions. And to date, every student I have taught has successfully made at least one bow, and most of them did it on their first try.

Before we go any farther on the discussion of making bows, we need to discuss tools. When it comes to making a bow, having the right tools is as important as knowing how to use them in the correct way.

Recently, my bowyer apprentice and I went to a five-day bow-shoot and bow-making event. We set up a booth and sold Osage orange, black locust, and honey locust bowstaves. Hundreds of people were there, and many were busy making bows and working on archery projects. As I wandered through the camps, I was shocked to see how many of the bowyers were using their drawknives upside down, with the dull side of the blade facing backwards. Many others had all kinds of pricey tools unnecessary to the craft. Most everyone was moving at what seemed a snail's pace to me.

I also saw bowyers so afraid to violate a growth ring that they were removing the layers of wood by scraping the back of the stave rather than drawknifing it. The more I walked around, the more people I saw using their drawknives upside down.

When I finally returned to our camp, I told my apprentice to go and look at the various bowyers making bows. I did not say anything about the drawknives or what I had seen. Instead, I got my workbench out of the trailer, attached a stave to the vise mounted on the end, and began to strip the stave down. It did not take long before several people had gathered around to watch me work. Finally, one man asked me why I had my drawknife turned the way I did.

"Because that's how the tool was made to be used. This way is the correct way," I replied.

The man said he had never seen anyone use a drawknife in that manner. I was dumbfounded, to say the least, and decided to put on a little demonstration. Picking up the pace, I took the six-foot bowstave down to a growth ring in about six minutes and then grabbed another. I had to chuckle as I saw everyone shaking their heads in disbelief at my speed.

The Warrior's Tools

After a while, my apprentice returned and remarked, "Did you see the way everyone is using their drawknives?"

"Yes." I smiled and kept on working.

Before the event was over that day, I had people standing in line to ask questions and request my help with their bows. It reminded me a little of my high school students patiently waiting to pose their questions as I went from one to another over the course of a class.

Do not let anyone make bow making too difficult.

To make a bow, you need nothing more than a good sharp drawknife, a wood rasp, a heavy-handled knife, the likes of a good twelve- or fourteen-inch butcher knife, a chainsaw file or small round file, and a variety of grades of sandpaper.

If you like, you can add a good sharp handheld hatchet for removing thick layers of wood from the belly of the bowstave, although I do not recommend this until you have made a few staves yourself.

I have made hundreds of bows with literally nothing more than those tools. You do not need all the various scrapers and other gizmos often shown in the bow-making section of archery catalogs. Most of those items are made to separate you from your money—they are not tools required to make a bow.

If you think you are going to make many bows, however, I would suggest at some point investing in a good-quality six-inch by forty-eight-inch belt sander with at least a one-horsepower motor. It will help you make bows must faster. I also have a fourteen-inch band saw but rarely use it for bows. It is mainly for cutting arrow shafts to length.

When working on a bowstave, you do need a good secure vise to hold it firmly in place. The vise can be mounted on a tabletop if the table is heavy and securely attached to the floor. You can also use a tree stump, a simple post planted in the ground, or something similar. The point is that you do not want the vise to be mounted on an unstable surface.

Another option is to make a simple bench and secure the vise to the end of the bench. Sit on the bench while working the stave, and your own body weight will keep the bench secure. Another benefit: the setup can be easily thrown into the back of a pickup or onto a trailer for mobile bow making.

The first step in making a bow is to make sure you are working with wood that is cured. When purchasing a bowstave, find out when the wood was cut, and make sure the person who cut it sealed the ends. A bowstave usually needs eight to twelve months of drying time before it is ready to be turned into a bow. If the wood has not been cut into a stave and is left in log form, be warned that it could take more than a year to cure.

Ideally, you want a bowstave that has as flat a back as possible, meaning that when you look at the end of the stave at the growth rings, you want those rings to be in straight lines wide enough to meet the width of the intended bow design. You do not want a bowstave that has growth rings rounded to the point that the back of your bow will be rounded. A flat-backed bow gives much more durability.

Growth rings vary in thickness depending on how much rain was received in each growing season. For a beginning bow maker, I would suggest harvesting or buying a stave with wider growth rings and a good straight grain.

When you look at a split stave from the side, the sapwood will tell you what the back profile of your bow will look like. If the sapwood is nice and straight, then the back of your bow will be nice and straight. If the sapwood is wavy, the back of your bow will follow suit. Always try to get a bowstave that has a nice straight line of sapwood running its entire length. That is visible while looking down the side of the split bowstave.

The Warrior's Tools

Many people give up on bow making after only a few attempts. I have seen it happen many times. It can usually be traced to two things: They either started out with inexpensive or poor-quality wood or they failed to harvest good material to begin with.

In my classes, I cut all the wood my students used for their bows and made sure each started with a superior bowstave. Better materials will cost more. In the long run, however, you have a better chance of success if you work with quality materials. It is much easier to work with a straight stave that has a few knots and wide growth rings than one that is twisted, full of knots, and tight grained. Leave such pieces until you first have some success with easier ones.

After you secure the stave into a vise, start by removing the bark from the entire length of the stave. Many people try to get right to the hardwood within the first couple of inches of the stave and then try to remove the bark and sapwood all at once. It might seem counterintuitive, but that is much more laborious than taking the layers off one at a time. If the stave is dry, the bark should flake off in big chunks. Once the bark is removed, you come to the sapwood layer. Take a moment at this point to look at the ends of the bow. You should see the difference between the sapwood layer and the hardwood layer. That is clearly evident in a rod of Osage orange because the sapwood is white and the heartwood, or hardwood, is yellow. In other woods, the variation is not as prominent, but you should see the distinction.

Start working at one end of the stave until you get a few inches of the sapwood removed. That should reveal the hardwood layer underneath. Work slowly but steadily with the drawknife, holding the blade's edge at just the proper angle to remove thin slivers of wood a little at a time. Once you get those first few inches of sapwood removed, work back and forth across the back of the stave to remove the rest of the sapwood evenly as you go.

When I am doing this, I often use my drawknife as a scraper, holding the blade at basically the same angle, but instead of pulling it toward me to cut wood away, I push it away from me, scraping back over what I just did to remove any small pieces of sapwood I might have missed. The drawknife is your multifunctional tool.

If you come to a knot on the stave, you want to work extra slowly. If you try to muscle your way through knots, they have a tendency to lift up large slivers of hardwood. Instead, work around the knot from various angles, slowly removing the sapwood right up to the very tip of the knot. I often use the extreme corner of the drawknife blade to remove the smallest layers of sapwood next to a knot. Knots are in all wood, and finding a stave without one is rare. Use sandpaper around knots to remove the last bits of sapwood, but do not sand so hard that you violate the growth ring.

After removing the sapwood, you might notice that the first layer of hardwood has what looks like streaks of sapwood in it. This is what I call an undeveloped layer of hardwood. If you encounter this, go down to the next growth-ring layer where the growth ring is a good even color. In some instances, you will have wood with dark streaks running in the growth ring. As long as the streaks are not actual cracks, you should be fine, in such a situation keep working.

There is no easy way to explain how to get down to a growth ring other than to have you get in the shop and work on a few staves. Your eye will soon begin to see where the layers change. Once you've taken a few staves down to the growth rings, you have mastered the hardest part of bow making. It's all fun going forward.

I am proud to say that all of my students have showed themselves to be fearless when it came to using their drawknives. Yes, at first, they were cautious, but once they could recognize the different layers of wood (and see the layer they needed to remove) and were comfortable with the drawknife, they got after it. Many of them violated a growth ring or two in the beginning and had to start over, but they regrouped and were not afraid to dive back in.

After only a few classes, usually no more than two-and-a-half hours long at a time, the majority of the students could get a stave down to a growth ring. By the end of the year, most of them could take a stave to a growth ring in fifteen to thirty minutes. Yes, I provided them with quality staves to begin with, but the only other tools I allowed were a wood rasp and a chainsaw file. The students had to remove all the excess wood by hand with a rasp.

Admittedly, that is by no means an easy task, but it teaches patience. When using a rasp to remove the wood from the belly and sides of the bow, a bowyer knows to move at a much slower pace, removing small amounts of wood at a time. By doing this, the bowyer is less likely to mess up along the way. Using a band saw or a hatchet is just asking to slip up and remove too much wood, thereby ending up with a nice piece of kindling instead of a bow.

Once the bowstave is worked down to the desired growth ring, I cut the stave to the length I want. Then using a yardstick, I find the center of the bow. I take a pencil and mark the center with a line and the letter "C," which stands for center. Then I determine the bow's shape and draw a straight line down the center of the bow. After your straight line is triple-checked, mark off a handle section of four to five inches. Most long bows have handles that are not true centers; the hand usually rests below center and the arrow pass is usually half an inch or one inch above center. That doesn't have to be the case with a shorter bow.

My short bows are usually held so the arrow passes about two inches to three inches above center, putting my hand more toward the center of the bow. If you make a longer bow, I suggest tillering the bow to where the arrow will pass half an inch to one inch above center. If a bow of fifty inches or less is made, make it two inches to three inches above center. If not, the limbs will have to be tillered a little differently to keep you from holding the bow pretty much on the bottom limb. Basically, the above will make a difference on how the limbs bend in a short bow but will not impact a long bow that rarely bends through the handle.

The next decision is marking the thickness of the handle with a pencil. A handle one inch to one-and-a-quarter-inches wide is good on a short bow. Use this same width the entire length for a squared-bow design or you can make the limbs of the bow a little wider and then taper them. I like a slight taper on my bows.

If you decide to go with a little wider limb and a tapered end, you need to measure one inch up from your handle and mark a straight line across the back of the bow with your pencil. If you have a one-inch-wide handle, measure a total width of one-and-a-half inches from the centerline that runs the length of the bowstave. If you have a one-and-a-quarter-inch-wide handle, measure one-and-three-quarters inches from the centerline. Then go to the tips of your bowstave and mark one-quarter inch on each side of the centerline.

Using the yardstick, hold it on the line that was marked one inch above the handle. Line it up with the mark you made at the tip on the same side and draw a line along the yardstick. Do this on each side and on the top and bottom limbs. You now have your bow drawn out nice and straight on your bowstave.

With your bow drawn out, it's time to use your wood rasp to start roughing it out. I have my students tighten the stave in a vise horizontally and rasp the sides of the bow. Hold the rasp vertically. Remove the wood with a straight up-and-down motion. Brace your body against the stave to hold the wood firm as you rasp. You want to continue to rasp until all you can see is the pencil line. Do not remove the line, but rasp up to it. Once this is done, use the rasp to reduce the wood on the belly of the bowstave. Attach the stave in the vise horizontally now with the belly facing upward. Start at the handle of the bow and work toward the tips, forming a gradual taper. Drawing a gradual tapering line on the side of the bowstave to the tip will give you a reference to the stopping point.

Make sure you leave plenty of wood, and do not rasp the wood too thin. The handle area should be thicker and the tips thinner. Hold your rasp flat across the belly of the bow when working. If you hold the rasp flat as you remove wood, you'll remove an even layer across the belly as you go. That is what you want. The belly of the bow should be flat, like the back, for maximum durability.

Once wood from the belly has been removed evenly from both limbs, you need to see if the bow is bending. I use a method called floor tillering. That involves putting the end of the bow on the ground. Then holding the bow at the handle with one hand and at the tip with the other, push down, forcing the bow to bend. You are looking to see if the limbs are starting to bend. Ideally, you want the limb to bend in a nice even arch. If the bow does not do that, you need to remove more wood until it does. The goal is to get both limbs to bend equally.

If an area is stiff and not bending, you need to remove more wood. Mark the offending spot with a pencil before putting the bow back in the vise. If you have a section bending just the way you like that no longer requires any more rasping, pencil off that section so you do not work it anymore. I have my students write the word good on the belly where they have a section that is bending nicely.

After you think both limbs are bending alike, take the file and make matching nocks on either end of the bow. That is not as easy as it seems. To be safe, mark half an inch down from the tip of your bow, and draw a straight line across the side of the bow tips. Then mark another line a quarter of an inch down from the first; that will ensure even spacing for your nocks. Hold your chainsaw file at an even angle between the lines where the bottom of the file touches the bottom line and the upper end of the file touches the upper line on the opposite side. Then rasp your groove for the nock. Repeat the process on the other side and the other tip to achieve a matching set of nocks. Nocks should be rasped into shape from the belly side of the bow, not the back. Nothing looks worse than a beautiful bow with nocks that are not even.

Now it's time to sand the sides and belly of the bow. Take a pencil eraser and remove all pencil lines from the back of the bow except for the one that marks the center of the bow at the grip.

After rough sanding your bow just enough to eliminate any splinters, brace the bow to see what it looks like. Tie the bowstring at the bottom end using a timber-hitch knot or clove hitch. The loop end should be at the upper end of your bow. For the first bracing, tie the brace height fairly low. Three to four inches is a good starting brace height. When the bow is braced, try to visually determine if the tiller in both limbs is the same or if one limb is bending more than the other.

If you have a limb that is not bending as well as the other, mark the limb with a pencil in the spot that needs to bend more. You can use your wood rasp if the limb needs to be adjusted a lot or your knife to scrape the belly if the adjustment is minor. After the wood is removed from the stiff limb, pull the string a few times, just enough to make the limbs flex. Then look at the bow again. If it is still off, make the necessary adjustments and repeat.

Once the bow looks good at low brace height, I suggest making your brace height five inches and putting the bow on a tillering stick. You want to make sure the center of the handle is in the "U" notch of the tillering stick before pulling the bow. If you place the bow setting off center in the tillering stick, your tiller will look off even if it is not. The one-inch-increment notches on the tillering stick should be marked from the base of the "U" notch according to length. If your first notch is ten inches from the "U" notch, then you know that is ten inches of draw length. Mark off all your notches so you will know the length from which you are drawing your bow and looking at the tiller.

If minor adjustments need to be made as you go, I suggest using your knife as a scraper and removing small amounts of material a little at a time. At this point, you are just fine-tuning your tiller. When using your tillering stick, be sure to know what the maximum draw length of your bow should be.

Do not try to overdraw the bow. If you have a forty-eight-inch bow, do not try to draw it twenty-eight inches. Realistically, you would be looking at a twenty- to twenty-four-inch draw length, depending on how much working limb you have.

Once the bow is bending evenly on your tillering stick, you can do your finish work and start to shoot your bow. I should note that finishing your bow will take some time if you do it right. I have seen so many nice bows that could have been excellent if the bowyer had just taken the time that proper finish work takes.

When the back of the bow is finished and it is down to a growth ring, all you need to do is make sure all your pencil lines are removed. Now you are ready to start sanding.

Start with a rough sixty- or eighty-grit sandpaper to make sure no rasp marks can be seen. Then graduate to a hundred-grit, then a 120-grit paper. Sand the sides and belly of the bow. Sand inside the nocks on the end to ensure that they are nice and smooth. I always like to remove the edges of my bow so they are a little bit more rounded than sharp. By doing this, if you ding the bow, it is less likely to put a dent in the wood that could cause a splinter.

Never use rough-grit sandpaper on the back of the bow—only use it only on the sides and belly.

If you want to go the extra mile, you should burnish your bow. Burnishing is running an object that is harder than the wood from which your bow is made over the bow, pressing down as you go.

Burnishing compresses the wood fibers and adds a lot of shine and smoothness. I usually use a smooth river rock that I have had since I was a small boy. Burnishing a bow can take an hour or two, but it is worth the end result.

Once your bow is finished, know that you should oil it often in the early years. Good sources of inexpensive oil are vegetable cooking oil, bacon grease, olive oil, or furniture polish oil. If you use bacon grease, heat it until it liquefies, pour it through a coffee filter, and then rub it liberally onto the bow. Wipe off any excess with a clean cloth.

Over time, by oiling your bow, you are protecting it from the elements. It will repel water, although the bow is not waterproof. The oil does, however, keep the bow from drying out, and that will add to its longevity. I have a self bow that was made in about 1991, and it still shoots as well today as when it was made because I have kept it oiled. As your bow ages, you will need to oil it only occasionally, but the bow should be oiled in the summer months when it is hot and dry.

Bows should be stored unbraced and either hung up or laid flat. Never stand a bow up in a corner like a guitar because this can put pressure on the bottom limb and cause the bow to come out of tiller or develop a twist. In some bows, a twist will develop after a bow is made, and that is because even in a good straight-grained stave, there can be some twist.

The best way to tell is to look down the end of the stave or bow and see if there is a twist. If there is, it can be removed with nothing more than a heat gun and a few C-clamps.

Again, it is not necessary to buy an expensive heat gun. Popular name brands can cost more than a hundred dollars. I purchased one of those once, and it lasted only five years. Today, I buy the generic ones that cost about eighteen dollars and last an average of two years—and I still come out ahead. When the heat gun I am presently using goes on the fritz, I will buy another generic one. C-clamps can be purchased at most hardware stores and cost only a few bucks each. It is good to have six or eight of these three-inch clamps on hand. You will also need a pair of leather work gloves.

When I have to heat-treat a stave, I lay it on my workbench, which has a square edge and a flat top. By laying the bow on its back so that it is flat up next to the straight edge, you can immediately see if the bow is straight, twisted, or both.

If it is twisted, you need to clamp the bow's handle right next to the straight edge of the table. I usually put a piece of thick buckskin between the clamp and the bow so I do not scar the wood with the metal clamp.

Now you are ready to straighten the bow by heating one limb at a time. After your handle is clamped into position, you need to clamp the limb that is not going to be heated. Do not try to force it straight. You are clamping it down only so that when you heat the other limb, the bow does not pivot at the handle when you pull it straight. Use one C-clamp midlimb and one at the tip. Next, use the heat gun on the first limb to be straightened.

Use the heat gun by holding it close to the wood, but keep it moving up and down the length of the limb—going over the back and sides, working from the handle to the tip or vice versa. If you are not moving the heat gun, you will see your wood start to turn dark. If this happens, you are getting the wood too hot. The wood needs to be heated throughout the entire limb to get the twist out without burning the wood itself.

A slight touch of the hand will let you know the wood is ready. If the wood is too hot to touch, it is ready to be clamped into position. Wearing gloves, take the tip of the bow and line it up with the edge of the table, then clamp it into place with a C-clamp. That should not be too hard to do if the bow has been heated properly.

Now clamp the bow at midlimb. You can then unclamp the clamps from the unheated side and follow the same steps. Once the bow is heated and clamped into position, you should leave the bow to cool for several hours.

When you unclamp the bow, the twist and crookedness in the stave should have been eliminated. If there is still a small amount of twist that remains or your bow is not perfectly straight, repeat the process. You should seldom have to treat a bow more than a few times.

And remember: Although bow making is hard work, it should be something done for enjoyment. If you find yourself becoming frustrated, stop, take a minute, and remember that this is a learning process. All skills have to be learned, and your skills will improve as you practice them. After thirty years of bow making, I still learn things all the time. You have to apply all that you have learned along the way if you hope to better your craft.

Occasionally, I still break a bow or violate a growth ring. Although rare, it does happen.

The old saying is true: "If you are not breaking bows, you are not making bows."

Chapter 4
Bending Bows to Shape

THERE IS MUCH DEBATE as to how Native Americans worked their bows into the various shapes we see in historical examples. As we discussed earlier, modern bowyers use a variety of methods to shape their bows, the most popular being heat and grease and steam.

Bowyers often also use a form or a variety of forms, often made of wood cut to the desired shape of the bend. Once the wood is heated with the heat gun and greased or steamed, the roughed-out bow is then put on the form and clamped into place with C-clamps and allowed to cool.

Once the wood is cooled, it is then unclamped, and the shape has been set into the wood.

As we consider the process from a Native American perspective, we should consider what methods best suited their lifestyle and the equipment they had at their disposal at the time. Through trade, the Plains tribes acquired many things that helped them with daily life, including tools that would have assisted in their bow and arrow making.

Military officers of the day kept records of items recovered from tribal camps after battle. The spoils included pots, kettles, frying pans, anvils, claw hammers, files, knives, axes, hatchets, and a wide variety of other miscellaneous things that the tribes itself had likely acquired through war, trade, or theft. Pots or kettles could be used to steam wood, axes to fell trees, anvils and hammers to pound out arrowheads from frying pans, and files to shape bows and sharpen points.

Grease was never difficult to acquire for the hunter-gatherer because every animal has fat, and fat is easily rendered into grease and a hot bed of coals is a good heat source.

Now that we see that the Native American bowyers of old could have used most of the methods we use today, we are left with the question of how they achieved the actual shaping of the bow because, to my knowledge, no bow forms or C-clamps have been found from that period in history.

Here is where we have to think outside the box a little.

As a youngster, my grandfather taught me to steam wood on an open fire with a kettle of boiling water. Once the wood had been steamed the desired amount of time, we simply inserted the steaming piece of wood into the fork of a small tree and applied pressure to easily bend the wood into shape. The downside was that we would have to stand for an extended period of time until the bow cooled off enough that the bend would set into the wood—or we had to use something to do that in our stead.

Another method for shaping wood calls for the steamed bow to be laid across a small log or stump and then weight to be applied to each bow tip, forcing the bow to bend. I have found that to be another easy and effective method. Bows could also be bent into shape by lashing them to a board and simply inserting a round one inch or two inches in diameter log under the section to be bent and using ropes to secure the bow into place.

All this being said—and despite having showed that it could be done in this manner—I am not 100 percent convinced this was the way people did it in the old days.

Rather, it is my thought that most bowyers on the Plains went a much easier route when bending their bows to shape. Many bows of old were made from branches of a tree rather than from cutting down a whole tree and splitting bowstaves from it, which is the most common method used today.

That is because in earlier times, it would not have been economical or practical to cut down an entire tree and drag bowstaves around with you for a year waiting for them to cure. The much easier path would be to cut a branch of about three to four inches in diameter that could easily be harvested with a hatchet and carried off on horseback. That approach makes a lot more sense given that the Plains people were a practical people.

One reason I believe that to have been the preferred method is because I have seen so many museum examples of Osage orange bows here in the Southern Plains that show the pith line on the belly, proving that the bow was made from a branch rather than a trunk. Osage orange, when growing, has a soft, spongy, pithy core that can easily be removed, leaving a distinct groove in the wood.

When a bow is made from smaller diameter branches, that pith groove is clearly visible on the completed bow. Those grooves are often misidentified by museum staff members as having been deliberately carved into the wood for some mysterious reason, whereas the actual reason seems to a bowyer like myself to be so obvious: The grooves are there because the bow was made from a branch.

The pith line is not visible when bow stock comes from larger pieces of wood. Seeing pith grooves on so many historical bow tells me that branches were probably also a wood source for bows on the Great Plains.

Smaller diameter bowstaves will also cure much faster than larger ones. The faster a piece of wood cures the faster a usable bow can be produced. I believe Plains bowyers would cut smaller staves and rough them into shape while green, grease them well to prevent cracking from drying them too fast, and then bend the wood to the desired shape while the wood was easily manipulated, and leave it to cure. That not only achieved the desired shape with little effort, but it also removed excess wood, reducing the curing time by months.

That raises the question of the bow being greased while drying. Many Plains bows were sinew-backed, and glue will not stick to grease. So we have to ask how a sinew-backed bow was made if the bow had had grease applied to it. Today, bowyers degrease their bows with dishwashing detergent or acetone. Historically, however, Plains bowyers used a simpler method that was equally effective. Their degreaser of choice was firepit ash and water. Bows were scrubbed with a mixture of ash and water several times. After the bow was dry, the bowyer could sinew-back the bow without worrying whether his glue would hold.

Having tried all of these methods myself, I am convinced that was the way most Plains Indian bows were shaped. As in all things, many paths lead to the same destination, but I always have to put myself in their shoes to see what would seem to be the most practical approach given the time and materials available. I urge you to try these methods yourself and draw your own conclusions.

Chapter 5
All About Sinew

SINEW IS ONE OF nature's most amazing materials. It can be used for many things, including sewing, making ropes and cordage, sinew-backing bows, and hafting (the process by which bone, metal, or stone is attached to a handle, or haft).

Native people harvested sinew from the many animals they hunted; the best sources were white-tailed and mule deer, elk, buffalo, antelope, and later cattle.

The two main sinews used were the backstrap sinews—that run along the back muscles next to the spinal cord—and the leg-tendon sinews. Sinew from the back legs was preferred because of its length, but all were used.

Both types of sinew, backstrap and tendon, work in almost the same way.

Backstrap sinew is scraped clean of any flesh and laid out to cure. It usually will harden within twenty-four hours and be ready for use. The sinew is easily separated from itself by twisting it in opposite directions until the fibers begin to separate. It can then be pulled apart into pieces as fine as modern-day thread.

Sinew is ideal for sewing, for making bowstrings, for tying down fletchings (the fin-shaped aerodynamic stabilization device on arrows), for hafting points to shafts or handles, and for reinforcing wrappings on bows or other weapons. It can also be used to sinew-back a bow, although I do not care to use backstrap sinew for that particular purpose.

Leg-tendon sinew is much harder to prepare and more labor intensive. Once the sinews are cut from the leg and any flesh is removed, the thick pieces of tendon take a little longer to dry. Once dry, the outer sheathing has to be removed to get to the sinews inside. The outer sheathing is best removed by placing the dried tendon on a hard surface and using a hammer and a pair of pliers.

Leg-tendon sinews are often greasy to the touch, but much of the oil is in the outer sheathing. When removed, the sinew within is usually not greasy. Once you start to pound the sinew with a hammer, the outer sheathing will begin to separate.

That is when I take the pliers and begin to pull pieces off until the sheathing is removed. The tendon sinew is much more fibrous than the backstrap. As the sinew is pulled apart, the webbing effect of the sinews can be seen. Tendon sinew has many more fibers per piece than does backstrap and so is ideal for backing a bow.

Some of the tendons are so thick that you can separate them into halves or fourths, providing ample amounts of prime sinewing pieces despite the labor involved in acquiring them.

Elk, buffalo, and cattle all have long leg-tendon sinews. The trick is getting someone who knows how to harvest it the right way. Otherwise, you can end up with short six- or eight-inch tendons when in reality you could have had twelve- or fourteen-inch tendon sinews. I have seen some cattle leg-tendon sinew as long as sixteen inches.

Pretty much all sinew from any animal is going to work in the same way. When you have separated it into workable pieces, you would be hard pressed to identify elk sinew from cattle or antelope from whitetail. I have tried various types of sinew from different animals and have seen no significant difference in the performance of the bows. However, I do see a major improvement when using tendon sinew versus backstrap.

The bows I have made of similar design and poundage using those two sinews proved that the bows backed with tendon sinew might slightly exceed the backstrap-sinew bows in distance and speed. On one such test, I had made a forty-nine inch Osage orange bow with a slight recurve at the last four inches of the tips, bent through the handle design one inch wide at the grip, one-and-a-half inches at the midlimb and half an inch at the tips. The small bow was fifty-two pounds at twenty-five inches and launched a dogwood Plains Indian–type arrow approximately six hundred grains in weight 198 yards, 203 yards, and finally 206 yards. I have yet to beat that with a similar design.

Anyone who knows bows knows that is a heck of a long way for a bow of such a design. In my experience, the average distance is roughly 160 to 180 yards. No flight arrows were used. Such sinew comparisons come from thirty years of bow making and with more than three hundred sinew-backed and other types of composite bows under my belt.

We will dive into sinew-backed bows, bow comparison, and design later on—for now, let's stay with sinew. When you buy processed sinew or if you process your own, you will have scraps too short for use. And just because you buy sinew already processed does not mean you will be able to use it right away. You usually have to separate it into desirable lengths and in matched bundles. You sometimes have to work out hard spots that the processor missed and pull off straggling pieces here and there.

I always trim off the ends of sinew pieces so they are squared off in each bundle. One bundle equals one piece, or section, of sinew backing. You should save all those scrap pieces until you have a large ziplock bag full. It might take a while, but all sinew is good for something. In this case, your scrap pieces can be used for making homemade hide glue.

Glue for sinew-backing a bow is critical.

In fact, it could be the deciding factor in not only your bow's performance but also its longevity. Many people nowadays look for shortcuts when doing almost anything, and too often that includes sinew-backing bows. Because of that, wood glue is often used as well as Knox gelatin and liquid hide glue. I have even seen two-part epoxy used. The problem with wood glue is that it will keep the sinew from doing its job by eliminating the stretch factor.

Hide glue allows sinews to stretch over the back of the bow. That is what gives the bow its extra whomp! Knox gelatin can be bought at the grocery store and comes in small packets with instructions. I have never used it so I cannot speak to its performance. Liquid hide glue has a retardant in it to keep it from drying too fast. It will remain sticky forever, not to mention that it smells like a wet dog. I am not even going to comment on epoxy. Good old granulated or homemade hide glue is the way to go. It should help that it is easy to make and not hard to find online. It is even rated in different strengths.

If you decide to make your own hide glue, there are many ways to do it. I like to cut up all my scrap sinew pieces with scissors until I have lots of small bits. When I have rawhide, I add rawhide scrapings into the mix, although sinew scraps alone are enough. The natural glue in the sinew needs to be extracted by boiling it in water. There is a lot of argument among bow builders on online web forums that boiling will not make glue, but I have done it for more than twenty years, and it works well for me.

Put your sinew in a large pan with enough water to cover the top of the scrapings. The pieces will begin to soak up water almost immediately, so it will most likely be necessary to add more water. Turn the burner on medium high and bring the pieces to a low boil, not a rumbling boil. As the sinew pieces begin to warm, the water will reduce. Occasionally, you will need to add more water over a three-hour period.

When the last water is added after about three hours, do not add any more. Turn the heat down to medium so that the water simmers but does not boil. Let the sinew pieces simmer on medium for the last hour. As the water reduces, you will see a caramel-colored soup form at the bottom of the pan; if you added rawhide to your mixture it will have shriveled to almost nothing. When the time is up and your wife has yelled at you for stinking up the house, strain the contents of the pot through a thin wire strainer, using a wooden spoon or spatula to press all the juice out of the congealed mess.

Once you have all the glue drained into a container, lay out a few baking sheets and pour the hot glue in a thin layer into the pan or pans. Within an hour or so, if the glue is congealed to a consistency like Jell-O, you have successfully made hide glue. If you poured the glue into the pan too thick, it will not harden before it starts to mold so the glue should be cut into squares, wrapped in foil, and put into the freezer. That will keep the glue until you are ready to use it.

If you poured the glue paper-thin, it will dry and harden, and you can break it into small pieces and store it in a ziplock bag until needed. Each bag of glue can be reconstituted by adding water and heating it in a double boiler or a hide glue pot.

Sinew has been described as oily and needing to be washed and degreased before it is used. I have purchased backstrap sinew several times that was oily, but that is not the norm when using leg tendon. If you get sinew that is greasy or oily to the touch, get it processed to the desired thickness for your project. Right before using it, rinse it in warm water with a liquid dish soap containing a degreaser. Then rinse it in fresh water until the soap is removed. That will degrease the sinew and leave it ready for use. Sinew will keep virtually for years if stored in a bag or container, as long as it is kept away from animals and bugs.

You should know that sinew is greatly affected by moisture. There is an old cavalry saying, "Indians won't fight in the rain." That is basically true, and for good reason. Most bowstrings were made from rolled sinew or spliced pieces of sinew twisted together to make a string long enough to brace the bow. When the sinew gets wet, it stretches. When it stretches, it comes unraveled. If you have a taut, twisted bowstring and it comes a downpour, your bow has just turned into a really nice club. Your arrow feathers get soaked, and then the water soaks into the sinew wraps holding the feathers down. All of a sudden, your arrows are featherless. Needless to say, it is no day to do battle.

When you get ready to sinew back a bow, you need to first prep your glue and sinew. I start by getting my homemade hide glue, or granulated hide glue, and putting it in a small six- or eight-inch round baking pan. Then I add warm tap water. The ratio for homemade glue should be about two parts water to one part glue. For granulated glue, the instructions will be on the package.

Put a larger pan on a stove burner and set on low to medium heat, fill with about two cups of water, and then set the pan with the glue on top of the pan of water. Basically, you have a homemade double boiler, although we are not going to actually boil the water. Instead, once you put the pan on the stove, wet a towel and wring it out so that it is damp but not soaking. Lay it on the workbench or counter where you are working. Then run your sinew bundles through warm tap water until they are soft and saturated with water. Run the pieces between your index finger and thumb to wring out any excess water. Lay the bundles on half of the wet towel and fold the other half over the top of them. That will keep your sinew moist. Leave the sinew in that condition for at least ten to fifteen minutes (this step is important because, as we noted earlier, sinew relaxes and stretches as it absorbs moisture).

With your sinew prepped and your glue on the stove, mix your glue (I like to use an old fork for this). Touch the glue with your fingers. It should be hot to the touch but not so hot that you cannot easily dip your fingers in it. If the glue is too hot, you will know instantly because the sinew will shrivel to nothing and be unusable.

Before applying sinew to the back of a bow, there are a few things you need to do to prep the bow. The main thing is to score the back of the bow. I recommend doing this before your sinew and glue prep. I do this with an awl and work in a crosshatch design the full length of the bow.

Some modern bowyers say scoring is not necessary.

Here is their argument: "Why would I violate the back of the bow by scoring it when I just spent all that time getting the bowstave to a single growth ring? With good glue, the sinew will stick to an unscored bow."

Yes, maybe, for a while.

But here is why the back should be scored. When you apply the sinew, it needs to have something to adhere to, but without being scored, the back of the bow is slick and smooth. Basic woodworking skills dictate that you need a rough surface when gluing things together, and scoring will not hurt the aesthetics or function of your bow.

Right before you begin to do the sinew-backing, run some hot hide glue over the bow first, like a coat of primer before a paint job. That layer of glue will soak into the scoring, fill in, and leave a layer on top of the scoring. Your sinew will adhere to that first layer of glue as you apply it, and as it dries, it will bond the back of the bow and the sinew into a single unit. I put my bow in a tabletop vise and do all my sinew-backing in the kitchen. I do, however, take the time to lay down some newspapers on the counter so that cleanup will be easier.

Nonetheless, you should be prepared for a smelly kitchen while you are working; the glue will have a bad odor while being heated. However, it will not transfer to the bow. Once the glue is dried, it will have no smell at all. I find it best to have the kitchen fairly warm. During the winter months when I sinew-back, I turn on the oven and open the oven door to warm the room before I start. I find it helps the sinew to dry faster on the bow.

When the glue is ready, it should not be thick but rather have the consistency of watered-down syrup. Take a bundle of sinew and dip it into the hot glue. Run it through the glue and then between your index finger and thumb to remove the excess. You want the sinew to be thoroughly soaked but not dripping with glue. I start at the tip of my bow, overlapping about one or two inches onto the belly side, and then right down the center to the handle.

I sinew-back bows one limb at a time. Once you have the centerline of sinew—from the tip to the handle, being careful to overlap the pieces about three-quarter of an inch—start to lay the rest down in a staggering bricklike pattern. You never want the pieces to butt up against each other but always overlap a little bit. If the progress is slow and the sinew is lifting a bit here and there, dip your fingers into water and run them over the back to smooth the sinew down and flat. Be sure to keep an eye on the glue to ensure that it does not get too thick. If that should happen, you might have to add small amounts of water, stirring and mixing the glue again.

Once I have sinewed one limb, I use waxed nylon cordage to wrap the whole limb, making the wraps about a half inch apart and pulling it firm, but not tight. That will ensure a good bond between the sinew and the wood, but it is only temporary. When laying down sinew, remember it is going to shrink as it dries. The shrinkage is what adds the tension and makes the bow shoot better. Do not be afraid to overlap the sinew side to side as well as end to end. Otherwise, you will have gaps, and you will have to go back to fill them in with more sinew eventually. That can be avoided by layering them well the first time.

When one limb is done, repeat the process on the other limb. When the sinew-backing is finished, put the bow in a warm place to dry.

After about three days, you will notice that the wrapping has started to come loose. That means the sinew is shrinking. You can then unwrap the bow. Add sinew wrappings to the tips and midlimb of the bow if you like. I always add at least one inch of sinew wrappings at the tips of my bows. The sinew wraps will help ensure that the sinew does not come loose at its weakest points.

In Oklahoma, where June, July, and August temperatures often tops 100 degrees Fahrenheit, I put my bows outside to cure during the day. In such conditions, a sinew-backed bow is cured enough to start shooting in seven to nine days. During the winter months, however, it can take as long as a month or two.

On sinew-backed bows made of good bowwoods, there is usually no reason to add more than one layer of sinew-backing. If you add more layers, you will have to wait longer for the sinew-backing to cure. I have heard and read over and over that you have to let a sinew-backed bow sit for at least six months before it is ready to use. That is rubbish! I have never waited that long. I start to shoot my bows whenever I think the sinew is cured. The sinew might continue to cure for several more months, but I have been known to start to shoot mine after a very short time and with great success.

The methods I have described here have worked successfully with hundreds of sinew-backed bows and should work well for anyone who wants to give it a try. By shooting your bow after it has set for as long as nine days in 100-degree F. temperatures, you will start to get the sinews stretching and pulling on the back of the bow. You are starting to give the bow its *memory*. In my opinion, that will help the break-in process. I usually consider a sinew-backed bow to be broken in after approximately five hundred to a thousand arrows have been shot through it. If something is going to happen, it usually will happen in that break-in period.

All things have pros and cons. For me, sinew has more pros than cons. The bow makers of the world who discovered and first used that amazing material figured out a system that has worked for thousands of years. It was natural glue, natural materials, patience, and an understanding of the process that it took to accomplish the desired result. Although modern man wants to improve on the ancient proven system of the sinew and hide glue, there has yet to be a man-made material that can surpass those natural materials when it comes to composite bows.

Sinew is the fiberglass of the ancient world and the not so distant past. I hope it will remain in use for generations to come. The materials are not hard to find, although it is hard to find people interested in learning the necessary skills to use them.

Chapter 6
Plains Indian Horn Bows
Part 1

IF SUCCESSFULLY MAKING a D-shaped self bow is elementary in bow making, then making a horn bow is at the college level, for sure. Several tribes used horn bows, but our discussion will be about the Plains Indian horn bow.

There are several reasons why horn bows were not seen on the Southern Plains: Bighorn sheep are not indigenous to the region, and the southern tribes do not appear to have cared to trade for such bows. They were presumably not only perfectly content with their native bowwoods, but also considered those materials were superior to those used by tribes farther north.

The southern tribes most certainly would have had the opportunity to acquire sheep horn from tribes to the west and the north through trade. They just didn't.

Horn bows have been the subject of great debate and speculation. Some people argue that such bows were not functional and were made more for ceremonial than practical use—this despite several documented accounts of early explorers having seen such bows being made and used. Having said that, I do find it difficult to believe any explorer or early writer witnessed every step of a horn bow's construction. Far more likely, such visitors witnessed a small part of the process and made notes on the parts witnessed.

Several surviving bows of the Plains Indian can be found in museums and private collections to this day. More than one, however, has been labeled as being made from cow horn rather than sheep horn. Bows made from elk antler are easier to identify, and there is no mistaking what they are made from.

My good friend Chuck Loffler, a fellow horn bow maker, makes a good argument that some cow horn can closely resemble sheep horn and that questions still surround the provenance of some horn bows.

I have yet to try to make a bow from cow horn, but I plan to in the near future and will do a comparison when finished. When it comes to the difference between horn and antler, just remember that horn is never shed but grows over the animal's lifetime, whereas an antler is shed and regrown annually.

I can recall one account of American buffalo, or bison, horn being used to make a bow. From what I understood, the pieces of that horn were glued to the belly of a wood bow rather than the entire bow being made of horn and sinew alone. That made sense, because even on a prize bull, the horns would not be long enough when spliced together at the handle to make a bow long enough for use.

Bows made from sheep horn and elk antler are quite short, usually thirty to forty inches in length. Some are made from a single antler or single horn rather than two horn pieces joined at the handle. Construction methods are debatable, but more than likely, only simple tools, such as a tomahawk or hatchet, knife, file or rasp, sandstones, and some sort of heat source, were used.

The Warrior's Tools

The process of making a horn bow would have taken the Indian bowyer many months. Even today with power tools, it takes me at least three months from starting to stringing the bow, and often even longer.

Why take the time? Perhaps it would help to know that the horn bow was so prized that one bow could be traded for as many as seven horses, it has been said.

As a well read bowyer of history, I had long been aware of the horn bows used by the Plains tribes but did not become very interested in them until I examined one from a friend's private collection. I was researching a few of his old Comanche bows when he showed me a horn bow made from wild mountain sheep. The bow was sinew-backed and reflexed. The sinew ran over the curved tips onto the belly for several inches. The tips were heavily wrapped with sinew and had a built-up nock made from sinew, and all the sinew was painted red. The bow also had a heavily stained white canvas grip wrapped with a buckskin thong.

I noticed right away that the bow had a modern bowstring, and I asked about it. The bow was documented to be more than two hundred years old and had been examined by a now deceased but leading archery historian who concluded that with a few repairs, the bow could be strung and shot. The expert had repaired the bow—to what extent I do not know—but according to the owner, the bow was strung and shot successfully with no ill effect. I did not get to measure the bow, but it appeared to be only about thirty-eight to forty inches long. The owner said the bow pulled more than eighty pounds of draw weight. After examining the bow, I made up my mind I was going to make a horn bow and see for myself if such bows were deservedly the stuff of legend or just ceremonial objects.

All the books I have read on the subject—by those who have tried to make horn bows and have successfully done so—explain the process to some degree, but having tried to follow in their footsteps, I found that many critical aspects were left out of the process.

"The devil is in the details," or so it is said. How very true!

If truth be told, I struggled with my first three attempts to make a sheep horn bow. I just could not get the exact process down, but with each mistake, lessons were learned and experience gained. By the time I started my fourth try at a sheep horn bow, I was pretty confident that I would succeed. That was a welcome feeling. Horns are not easy to come by and are expensive. It is also important to make sure the horns have been harvested legally and can be sold legally.

I am often asked about other species of sheep that might make for a fine modern horn bow. Although most species of sheep have horns comprised of exactly the same material, not all sheep horns are feasible for making horn bows. Sheep such as the mouflon of Sardinia and western Asia have too much curl in their horns. Their horns are also generally not long enough or wide enough to make a good horn bow. The horns of Alaska's Dall sheep and bighorn sheep, however, are ideal for bow construction.

When making any bow that represents a people's culture, I believe you should try to be as historically accurate as possible; this honors the culture and the people.

On a more practical note, a set of horns intended for making a horn bow should have as little damage as possible. Cracks or splits around the outside curl of the horn can run several layers deep, and they could cause problems with the bow later on. I also always try to find a pair of horns without a lot of twisting curl. A nice sweeping curled horn works much better than one with wide flaring curls. The ideal length of each horn should be no less than twenty inches around the outside curl. However, if you can find a longer horn, you will have more material to work with, and in this case, more is better.

Once the horns are acquired, mark the outside curl of the horn with a marker. Then mark each side of the outside curl of the horn as wide as you can possibly get it from the base of the horn to the tip. There will be a gradual taper in your line as the horn gets narrower toward the tips. You can use masking tape to help mark the lines straight by taping off the horn along the curl and then drawing a line down the edge of the tape.

When that is done, the inside curl of the horn has to be removed. Removal is a tedious process that needs to be done with care. Be sure to wear safety glasses while you work. Using a handsaw or hatchet, remove the horn a little at a time. I prefer to use a handsaw because the natural curl of the horn makes it almost impossible to cut out on a band saw. If you slip, you will ruin the horns in a hurry. You should reap some good pieces of horn from the sides and inside curl that will come in handy later in the construction process.

Once the inner curl of the horn has been removed, secure the horn in a vise. A wood rasp is ideal for squaring up the sides of the horn and smoothing down the inside of the curl. Once all the cut marks have been smoothed out from the inside curl and the horn has been squared up to your line, start to rasp the outside curl, removing all the ridges in the horn. If you have a belt sander, you can complete this step much faster, but you have to be cautious and move at a much slower pace. You do not want to sand through a horn; instead, you want to make it nice and flat so the entire outer surface is smooth to the touch.

After the horn is squared and rasped smooth on each side, you want to straighten the horns. I do not boil horns, preferring to soak them in water that is *almost* boiling. Boiling can damage the horn—or risks damaging it. A large pot or a basting pan will work fine for this step. You will need twenty to thirty C-clamps and a straightedge board wide enough to clamp both horns to.

When the water is steaming but not boiling, submerge one horn into the pot and let it soak for twenty minutes. You will notice that the horn's curl will become more pronounced while in the water. While the horn is soaking, get your C-clamps and straightening board ready. Once the horn is removed, you will have only a short amount of time to clamp the horn to the board. The horn will begin to cool and stiffen as soon as it is removed from the hot water. I always begin by clamping my horn aligned with the edge of the board, and I like to start at the base of the horn—putting a clamp every two inches until I get to the tip. As you clamp the horn, you will need to pull on it to align it with the straight edge of the board.

After one horn is clamped into place, repeat the process with the other horn. Leave the horns to dry for twenty-four hours. When you unclamp the horns the next day, they should have lost about 90 percent of their curl. This is the time to make sure the horns stayed fairly straight. If not, repeat the process again until they do. When the horns are nice and straight, you will notice that they remain somewhat flexible. Do not try to force them to bend too much at this state. The inside part of the horn will end up being the back of the bow, and the outside curl will end up being the belly. That will force the horn to bend against its own natural curl and make for an awesome natural reflex that will be deepened with layers of sinew.

Remember that the base of the horn will be thin, which is why several inches should be removed up to the spot on the base where the horn starts to thicken. Both horns need to be the same length. Because the two pieces of horn will be joined at the handle in one of several ways, the bow can be up to five inches shorter than the total length of the horns. Before you can decide the bow length, however, you need to decide how the horns will be joined at the handle.

A common Plains Indian method overlaps the two pieces four to five inches at the handle and then uses a piece of horn to cover the overlap on the top and bottom of the handle. The handle is then glued together. After boring holes through the horn with a hot awl or another small drill, the bowyer would use copper rivets or pins made from horn or wood to secure the handle in place. If that method is used, remember that you will end up with a bow several inches shorter than the total length of the horns.

I favor a traditional method that calls for a "V" splice. One horn is cut at the center of the base and a section of horn is removed, leaving a V-shaped cutout. The other horn is trimmed to fit into the cutout, resulting in a spliced joint. The splice is held together with hide glue, and then an upper and lower horn piece is made to cover the splice and is pinned or riveted to secure it. This method will shorten your bow only slightly, depending on how deep you make the splice. A splice of only three inches deep is plenty big enough.

There were a few more methods used by Indian bowyers, but in my opinion the ones mentioned here have proved to be the safest and most durable.

Having decided which handle you want, cut the horn to an acceptable length but not shorter than forty inches. If the length of your horn is already less than that, don't worry about shortening it. If you do need to trim the horn, remember that you want to do it at the base, not the tip.

With the horn cut to the desired length, use a pencil to mark the actual bow on the horn. If you left the horn as wide as you could, it will be too wide and will need to be narrowed somewhat. Then overlap the two horn pieces at the handle three to five inches, depending on what method you are using to join the two pieces together. Use a C-clamp to hold them together at the center and then decide the width of the handle.

A good handle width is one-and-a-quarter to one-and-a-half inches. I like limbs of a horn bow to be wider, so I usually make them one-and-three-quarters to two inches wide at the midlimb and then start the taper toward the tip. The tip of the horn will already be narrow, so simply make a gradual taper from the midlimb to the tip. After all your lines are drawn on both limbs, rasp off the excess horn or use a belt sander, which will be much faster.

When you have the horns nicely shaped, begin to work the limbs down to a thickness that will bend easily in the hand. Use a rasp for this, filing the horns to the point that you can easily flex them. Test this by holding the tip with one hand and the base with the other.

Because you are working on two individual pieces—and each piece is a limb of the bow, you are almost constructing two bows given that you have to tiller each horn exactly the same. Once the back of the horn is worked smooth with no remnants of ridges, remove the rest of the material from the inside curl or belly of the limb to achieve tiller. You will not know how close they are until you join the handle together.

To construct the overlapping handle, decide which horn will lie on top and which will lay on bottom. The two pieces need to be worked enough so that they will lie against each other flush, with little if any gap. This step is critical to the success of the bow because the handle is a bow's weakest point.

Once the two pieces are ready to be joined, be sure to mark with a pencil exactly where the overlap should be positioned. With an awl, score the two horns with a crosshatch pattern; that is where they will be glued together. The scoring will help the joint hold more securely when glued.

Next, with your hot hide glue, liberally coat each side of the horn in the scored section where the horns will be joined. Once they are glued, position the horns together, using several C-clamps to hold the joint in place. I usually wait twenty-four hours and then go back and apply more hide glue to any gaps I see along the edges of the joint.

If you choose to make the bow with the "V" splice, make sure the cut for the splice is centered on the handle where the tip of the "V" cutout is perfectly centered in the middle of the bow. If it is not centered, you will likely end up with a bow that not only has one limb off-center but is also unable to be braced without twisting in the hand.

After cutting the "V" splice, next cut the other limb so that it will fit perfectly into the splice. Again, use hot hide glue to coat the inside of the "V" splice and the part of the other limb that will fit into the splice. After you join the two pieces, use several C-clamps to clamp the bow on the outside of the joint, forcing the joint to close tightly. After twenty-four hours, you can add more glue to the joint to fill any gaps.

While the splice or overlap is drying, make the horn plates that will cover the handle on the top and bottom. The plates add stiffness and support to the handle of the bow. I use the leftover pieces from the side of the horns that were cut away earlier. If you used the three-inch "V" splice, you will need two pieces of horn the width of the handle and four to five inches long. If you used the overlapping method, you will need two horns five to six inches in length, depending on the length of your overlap. The pieces need to completely cover the handle and at least half an inch on either side of the joint or overlap. I have found that a full inch is even better.

The horn pieces need to be as flat as possible yet flexible enough to bend in the hand. I cannot give you a set thickness because some horn pieces have to be thinner than others. The pieces also need to have a little flex because they will need to follow the curve of the back and belly of the bow. Once the horn pieces are worked to size, thin a nice taper to the ends and round off the edges. After the handle section has set for at least a week, it is okay to carefully unclamp it—but do not try the bow. This is not the time to flex the bow because the joint is not yet reinforced and thus is quite weak.

The completed horn pieces will be centered on—and will cover—the handle area of the bow. Mark the one-inch overlap on each side of the splice position with a pencil. When the pencil marks are aligned, score the horns on the side that will be glued to the belly and back of the handle. Also score the area between the pencil lines. You will use the same crosshatch scoring pattern as before. When finished, apply hot glue to the horn pieces and to the bow. Once you have the horn pieces in place, use several C-clamps to hold them in position. The pieces need to stay clamped in position for a week to ensure a good bond. Check it in twenty-four hours and again fill in any gaps in the glue line.

After the handle section has set for a week to dry, unclamp it, but again, do not put any pressure on the bow because the handle will still be weak. If you try to flex the limbs, your new horn pieces are likely to pop off.

Next, choose horn, wood pins, or copper rivets to secure the handle into position. Mark three to five evenly spaced circles on the horn pieces that cover the handle. Make sure that the ones closest to the end are away from the edge just enough so that the rivet or pin will not crack the horn piece. If you get the hole too close to the edge when tapping the pins or rivets into place, you could crack the horn and have to start all over on a new piece.

Once the holes are marked, drill them out using a bit slightly smaller than the pin or rivet being used. Doing this will ensure a nice snug fit. The holes should be drilled all the way through and sanded to remove any burrs that might have popped up at the entry or exit of the drill bit. If copper rivets are used, tap them into place with a hammer, and then lay the bow on a hard, flat surface and put the rivet burr into place. Hit the end of the rivet until the head flattens, securing everything.

If you make pins of wood or horn, fill the holes and coat the pins with hide glue before tapping them into place. The pins should be longer than the holes. Remove any excess with a small handsaw once the pins are set. If you use copper rivets, you are ready for the next step. If you used pins, they need to sit and dry for three or four days before you proceed to the next step.

The bow is now at a point that it can be held by the tips and flexed to a small degree. Horn is great in compression but weak in tension, so it will feel flimsy and weak. The tips of the bow need to be curled over toward the back of the bow. The curls will eventually be wrapped with sinew and become the nocks that hold your bowstring.

I use a heat gun and a pair of pliers to bend the tips. Start by heating the bow tip until you can easily bend it with the pliers. You need to bend only the last half inch to three-quarters inch of the tip. Know that it will take only a few seconds to get the tip hot enough to bend. Once you bend the tip, hold it into position for several minutes until it cools enough to hold the shape. Once it has cooled, you can carefully brace the bow and have a look at the tiller at brace height.

At this point, your bow will be easy to string. With string in place, the bow can also easily have one limb straightened and the other bent in a huge arch. The bow will be unstable, so be very careful.

If the tiller is close, once the bow is braced, it should hold the string with no problem. You can tell right away if the tiller is off and if one limb is stiffer than the other. If that is the case, mark the stiff area with a pencil, unstring the bow, and try using steam to bend the bow limb to the correct tiller. Be careful not to get the steam close to the handle joint. If the tiller cannot be achieved with steam, use a knife to scrape the stiff sections a little at a time, continually restringing the bow and checking. Getting your tiller close will save you a lot of work in the later stages of this project.

When you are satisfied with the tiller of the bow at brace height, score the entire back of the bow with the awl. The scoring should be in a crosshatch pattern and deep enough to feel rough to the touch. Now you are ready for the first layer of sinew.

I prefer leg-tendon sinew to backstrap sinew, as mentioned earlier, but either will work. I lay my first layer of sinew on the bow and overlap the sinew to cover the sides of the bow as well. Next, wrap the whole bow from tip to tip with waxed nylon cord, securing the sinew to the bow. Because sinew shrinks within three days, the cord will become slack, and you will find you already have some reflex in the bow.

Before you add the second layer of sinew, sand the first layer, making sure to remove any residual wax left from the cordage. Then add the second layer of sinew right over the first and wrap the bow again. The cordage will become loose again in a few days and then can be removed. The second layer should dry two weeks before you add the third. Once the third layer of sinew is added, you will notice that the bow has gained more reflex. The third layer should also dry for two weeks before you add the fourth layer of sinew.

The fourth layer of sinew might end up being the last or one more layer might be required to get the poundage you want. I have been known to put as many as six layers on a horn bow and as few as three. Once the final layer is applied, I wrap the bow with cordage and leave it alone for at least a month to dry.

When the month has passed, your bow will have gained more reflex—a lot more. It is time to start flexing the bow, bending it by putting the handle on your knee and pulling the limbs toward you. Be very careful. If the bow is highly flexed, it will try to twist on you. And remember: You do not want to pull the bow extremely far, just to where brace height will be. If the bow feels heavy and has a lot of resistance, you probably do not need another layer of sinew. If it is easy to bend, add another layer of sinew to up the poundage.

Once you are satisfied with the bow, it is time for the sinew wrapping. This step is not for decoration but for reinforcement. At this stage, the bow will be highly flexed and under a huge amount of tension when braced, so you need to add a two-inch sinew wrapping at the tips. The entire handle should be wrapped with sinew at least one inch past the handle section on each limb. The curl that was put in the ends of the bow also needs to be wrapped with sinew and made to the point that a string can fit around it. Although the bow has no nocks in the tips, the curved tip you bent over and covered with sinew is more than sufficient for nocks.

The bowstring will be attached to the bottom with a bowyer's knot or timber hitch, and the top, with a slipknot. Some bows will gain more reflex than others. If I have a bow that is extremely reflexed, I usually straighten it out a bit before stringing. I clamp the bow at the handle to a workbench or premade form. Then I pull the limbs down even with the table and clamp the tips down, basically clamping the bow to the table. I usually let the bow stay in that position overnight. After unclamping it the next day, I string it. That will make the stringing process a little bit easier. It does not hurt the bow, and it will regain the reflex shortly after unstringing.

You can carefully brace the bow with the step-through stringing method. Be sure to hold the bow firmly and keep the handle of the bow centered exactly against the back of the knee. A bow once blew up on me while I was stringing it in this manner because the handle was not centered on the back of my knee but rather higher up on the upper limb. When I bent the tip around to slip the string around the nock, I heard an explosion and felt a severe kick. The upper limb snapped into two pieces. Luckily, the sinew kept the bow together, preventing further injury to me. Since then, I have always worn safety glasses while stringing a bow.

When you string the bow at first, it might look slightly out of tiller. If so, don't panic. This often happens on the first bracing and even many times later. It just means that the bow needs to sit for a while and adjust to the string. Often after a few short tugs on the string, the bow will come into tiller. If not, you can adjust the tiller in one of two ways.

Here is where the debate begins.

I bring my horn bows into tiller by scraping fine layers off the belly of the bow with a pocketknife until the limbs balance out. I have read that is not the *proper way* to tiller a horn bow. That might be true, but I have done it many times, and it has always worked fine for me.

The other option, which is considered the *right way*, is to add sinew to the weak limb. As the sinew dries, it will add more tension to the weak limb, thus making it stronger and making the bow come into tiller. I have used this method, but if you have to go back and add more sinew, you will also have to wait another week or two for it to dry. Then, say, you have to add a little more, and that week turns into more weeks. Instead, by simply scraping the belly of the bow, you can get the tiller adjusted in a matter of minutes.

Once the bow is bending correctly, you can polish the horn belly with a white polishing compound or jeweler's rouge and buffing wheel. Either will make the horn shine and look stunning. Next, add the final sinew wraps at the midlimbs of the bow. The wraps need to be two inches and centered in each limb. The sinew wrapping at the tips, midlimbs, and handle are for reinforcing the bow and are a necessity.

After making six sheep horn bows, I have found the bows to be more than sufficient to harvest any animal in North America. I have made horn bows with forty-two to sixty-five pounds of draw weight. Such bows are smooth and fun to shoot. Maybe that's why I feel confident that the horn bows made by the Plains Indians in previous centuries were not used only in ceremonial rituals but as tools for hunting and warfare.

The weeks it can take to make a horn bow can add up. After months of working on a horn bow, I have often asked myself why any Indian bowyer would take all that time to make such a bow when suitable bowwood was at hand and was much, much easier to work with.

My conclusion: Why not?

The truth is that it is human nature to create, and the bowyers of the past, just like bowyers today, appreciate the variety of bow styles—and the challenges they offer.

That said, I know of only one other person besides myself who is making traditional Plains Indian horn bows. Our methods vary somewhat, but the end result is the same. I am confident that all the old Indian horn bowyers used methods of construction similar to ours. I also suspect that each had his own way of doing things, so I would say the right way to make a horn bow is the way that works best for you.

Chapter 7

Plains Indian Horn Bows
Part 2

ELK ANTLER BOWS ARE constructed using many of the same methods used for sheep horn bows, but they are much easier to complete and have fewer tedious steps in their construction. I have never seen an old Indian-made elk antler bow, but I have seen many pictures and specifications of old bows. After having read what little I could find about them, I decided to make one.

The elk antler bows I researched were like sheep horn bows in many ways. Several were very short, less than thirty-five inches, and were constructed of only one horn, whereas others measured in the upper-thirty-inch range and were constructed of two horns.

I decided to make a two-piece bow. To do so, I needed a pair of antlers that had just the right curvature and were straight enough to make one bow limb from each antler. I searched the Internet until I found just what I was looking for—a set of elk sheds for less than two hundred dollars, a good deal compared with what mountain sheep horns cost.

I knew antler was much easier to work with than sheep horn because I have made numerous elk antler arrowpoints. While waiting for the antlers to arrive, I prepared a dozen sinews from elk leg tendon sinews and a few backstrap pieces and started to ponder the makings of the bow.

When the horns arrived, they were just as I had hoped. Each main beam had a nice sweeping curve, plenty long enough for a bow limb. I sawed off the tines and other points and cut out each section of main beam that was destined to be my limb. Each section was cut to twenty inches long. With my six-inch-by-forty-eight-inch belt sander, I then began to remove the inside of the curve that would form the back of the bow, thinning the antler from base to tip until the porous center pith of the horn was visible.

I took the sander to the outside of the horn—what would become the belly of the bow—and sanded just enough to remove the outer layer to make the horn somewhat flat. At that point, I drew the desired shape of each limb in pencil on each antler one-and-a-half-inches wide at the handle, flaring to one-and-three-quarters inches midlimb, tapering to half an inch at the tips.

Then it was back to the sander so I could square up the limbs to the pencil lines.

When I was finished, I was surprised that in only an hour, I had both antlers roughed out and flexing in the hand.

Then I had to decide what kind of handle splice to use. I was looking at the two limbs and the pile of excess antler lying on the floor when I noticed a piece of antler that had a nice shallow "C" shape about as thick as the handle of a baseball bat. I cut the section of antler to five inches in length and worked it roughly to a shape an inch-and-a-half wide by an inch-and-a-half thick throughout, being sure to keep the curvature.

I measured the center of the five-inch section, marking it at two-and-a-half inches, which was the center point. Then I drew a thick line two inches long by one-half inch (a half inch was the thickness of the base of the antler limbs) onto each end and both sides of the C-shaped piece. Using a band saw, I carefully cut out the grooves and sanded them inside to make each smooth. Next, I slid each antler into the base of the grooves to see how they would fit. To my surprise, they fit well.

Because the C-shaped piece of antler had the ends pointing upward, it gave the profile of the bow some induced reflex. Basically, I had just made a bow with a setback handle, which should give me a bow with a gull-wing shape, or so I hoped.

I realized at the time that this was more than likely not the way the Plains Indians joined their elk antler bows together. However, I was confident that my way would allow for a more secure handle joint and make the bow more secure at its weakest point, which again is at the handle. One thing I knew for certain: This was definitely an improvement on the original method.

I used hide glue to secure the horns into the handle section of antler and clamped them together using a C-clamp on each joint. After twenty-four hours, I went back and added more glue to the outside of the joint to ensure a good glue line.

After a few days, I unclamped the handle. I drilled a hole in the center of each joint all the way through and made two wooden pins from dogwood, dropped hide glue into the hole, and smeared it over the dogwood pins before tapping them into place with a rubber mallet. I then let the pins dry for three or four days. At that point, I was excited about my swift progress with the elk bow. I was weeks ahead of schedule in comparison to making a sheep horn bow.

I used a rasp to work the back of the bow until it would flex a little bit, but I noticed the antler was stiffer than sheep horn. That told me I would more than likely need fewer layers of sinew. My antlers were about a half-inch thick from the base of the limb all the way to the last few inches of the tips, where they became a little thinner.

It was then that I noticed the bow looked a little long, and I decided to measure it. It measured forty-one inches along the curve. Wanting to stay within what I thought was a good length for a horn bow, I cut an inch-and-a-half off each tip, shortening the bow to thirty-eight inches overall. I reworked the tips, and using heat, slightly bent over the last half inch of the tip-top of each limb.

So far, I had been impressed with the ease of construction—on heating to straighten, no clamping the bow into position. There was also no difficult handle overlap or splice joint to deal with. The antler bow was much easier to make than the sheep horn bow thus far.

I sanded the remaining pith from the back of the bow by rolling sandpaper around a wooden dowel and using it to sand inside the pith groove. Using my awl, I scored each limb from where it emerged from the handle all the way to the tip. I also sanded the section of the handle where each limb protruded until there was a nice smooth taper from handle to limb. I scored the back of the handle and laid down the first layer of sinew on the back of the bow, overlapping each tip the sinew went around and making sure to cover two inches of the belly.

I also applied a layer of sinew to the sides of the bow and then wrapped the whole bow with waxed nylon cordage from tip to tip. After three days, the cordage loosened somewhat as the sinew shrank. I removed the cordage and allowed the sinew to dry for a few more days.

When I was ready to add the second layer of sinew, I noticed that the bow had not gained much, if any, reflex, as sheep horn bows do. Perhaps that was because the antler is denser than the horn and thus requires more sinew to induce reflex. I laid down the second and third layers back to back and then wrapped the

The Warrior's Tools

bow with cordage and allowed it to dry for four weeks. When the sinew was cured, the bow had again gained only a small amount of reflex, but sinew continues to cure for as long as a year, and usually more reflex is gained over time.

I reinforced the nocks and the entire handle section with extra sinew wrappings. Wearing safety glasses, I braced the bow. To my great surprise, the bow was almost in perfect tiller. I pulled the bow a few times and could tell it had a lot of power.

I scraped one limb slightly with my pocketknife until the bow's tiller was spot-on. I added more reinforcing sinew to the midlimbs and colored all the wrappings with green ochre. For the sinew along the back, I used a rusty red color. I added a smoked-brain-tanned handle and wrapped it with a buckskin thong. The bow was finished, and I was more than ready to test it. I knew with a five-inch handle and one inch of horn secured in the base of each handle on each limb, I had only thirty-one inches of working limbs. In wood-bow terms, I would only be able to draw the bow only fifteen-and-a-half inches if the tiller was spot-on.

Because of my experience with sheep horn bows that can draw several inches beyond what they theoretically should do, I was positive that my new elk bow would draw much farther. The reasoning behind that theory was that horn and antler are good in compression, and the sinew adds tremendous tension.

That combination should allow for what is called overdraw.

Being a little skittish about the bow's capabilities, I slowly tested the bow, thinking that it had all been way too easy, and something had to go wrong. I marked fifteen-and-a-half inches on an arrow shaft and cautiously pulled the bow to that point. When I got there, I heard no ticks, creaks, or cracks—sounds often heard before a bow breaks.

Instead, the bow was springy and surprisingly smooth.

I decided to pull it some more.

When I reached nineteen inches of draw, I felt the bow was at its limit and, like the draw, just stopped. The bow was maxed out.

I put the bow through its paces over the next few weeks, shooting it every day. The more I shot it, the better it seemed to shoot. The bow was pulling close to fifty pounds at nineteen inches of draw with three layers of sinew backing—impressive, for sure. I eventually reluctantly sold the bow to a customer who made me a price I could not refuse.

Over the years, I made several more elk antler bows with great success and little failure. I believe the perennial success came from being extremely picky about the antlers I used. Old sheds or antlers that have been lying around too long might become too brittle for a good bow. Antler can break just like wood or horn—another reason why patience is key when making a bow.

The handle section I devised ended up working so well that I used the same method for all the elk antler bows I made. I tried various handle shapes, even flipping the "C" shape the other way, although the results were not so good. The bow came out as a deflexed handle and reflexed limb. That did allow for longer draw length by pushing the handle forward instead of back toward the shooter, but I found the overall shape of the bow not to be pleasing to the eye.

Having mastered the antler horn bow, I was now ready to try my hand with buffalo horn. I ended up making a dozen bows of that type. One landed on the pages of a prominent archery magazine.

The Plains Indian bow of buffalo horn, or bison horn, is a bow that I have never seen firsthand and have never seen in a photograph—and I can recall having seen only one written reference to a bow of that type.

It seems that the bow was constructed by placing sections of buffalo horn to the belly of a wooden bow and gluing them into place. That seemed feasible to me because I know that horn adds compression. It seemed reasonable for horn to be added to the belly of a bow that was naturally weak in compression. It would make the bow more durable. Still, I fought with myself over the idea of the historic need for such a bow. All the Plains tribes had decent bowwood in their territory and if for some reason they didn't, they could certainly trade for it.

Why would a bowyer go to so much work to make such a bow? Again, it was an question I was determined to answer.

I started the process by locating six sets of buffalo horn caps. I bought sets that were labeled extra large, and in short order, they arrived. As I looked over the horns, I noticed that the largest sections were on the outside curl and ranged from a foot to fourteen inches. I first cut off the tips of every horn a few inches down from the tip. The tips of the horns are narrow and solid and not usable. Then with a silver marker, I marked out a section as wide as I could from base to tip along the outside curl. I then cut out the horns on a band saw sideways, removing the inside curls.

With all the horns cut, it was time for the sander. I squared the pieces to one-and-a-half-inches in width. Some of the pieces had to be shortened on the tips to meet the desired width. I sanded each horn to have a perfectly squared-off end. When finished, I had pieces ranging from seven to nine inches in length. I then sanded the horns flat on each side until they flexed in my hand and were an even thickness throughout.

All the pieces still retained their natural curl. Just like on the other horn or antler bows I had made, I decided that the outer curl would be the side for the back of the belly and the inner curl for the belly of the wood bow core. I made an Osage orange bend-through-the-handle D-shaped bow forty-eight inches in length and one-and-a-half inches wide throughout, a squared bow with a perfectly flat belly of forty pounds draw weight at twenty-four inches. In a crosshatch pattern, I scored the belly of the bow and each horn piece with an awl, marking the center of the bow with a pencil. I also marked one of my longest pieces of buffalo horn in the center.

The next step was to apply hot hide glue to the entire belly of the bow and brush a layer on the piece of horn. Then I centered the horn on the center mark on the bow's handle and clamped the horn into position with as many C-clamps as I could fit onto the piece of horn. I glued another horn and butted it up next to the first one so the squared ends met in what is called a butt joint.

I clamped the next piece of horn in the same manner, with it butting up to the end of the first piece. I did this until I reached the end of the limb, where I had a piece of horn hanging off. Then I applied horn to the other limb in the same manner. I had dozens of C-clamps holding the horn into position and decided it had better sit to dry for at least a few weeks.

I had never worked with horn and wood together before, so I wasn't sure how long it needed to dry, but I wanted to be on the safe side. After a few days, I used a small paintbrush and, working around the C-clamps, managed to get more glue into a few spaces where I could not see any between the horn and the wood belly of the bow. The horn pieces dried for ten days before I unclamped them. I cut the excess horn pieces that were extending outward past the tips flush with the ends of the bow and narrowed the tips to a half inch on the belt sander.

I was already calculating whether my horns were an even thickness and whether the bow would still be in tiller when I finished. I was tempted to try to brace the bow, but experience told me that without any sinew wrappings to secure the butt joints, I had better not.

In my usual method of construction, I sinew-backed the bow, but I also ran the sinew over the sides of the bow and covered the very edge of the horn pieces on the belly. After a few days, the sinew seemed dry enough that I could add the sinew wrapping to each butt joint. I completely covered each joint with a one-inch-wide sinew wrap, and then I wrapped the tips of the bow for several inches on each end. I let the bow set for another week before cutting the string nocks with a chainsaw file.

The moment of truth was at hand.

It was time to string the bow.

As I slipped the loop over the upper tip of the bow and slid it down several inches, I secured the bottom with a timber hitch and stepped through the bow to brace it. As I bent the upper limb around, I found I could not slip the string into the nocks. The bow was much stronger than I could have ever imagined. I took a deep breath and with all the effort I could muster, I managed to get the string into the nocks. I plucked the string to listen to the bow, and it made a high pitch twang. At that sound, I knew the bow was going to be much stronger than the forty pounds it had started out at.

The first few times with the bow, I pulled the string slowly and only about ten to twelves inches before trying to come to a full draw, which would have been twenty-four inches. Each time, I struggled to draw the bow fully—I guessed the draw weight to be ninety pounds. I had to stop and scratch my head for a few minutes. I knew the sinew would add a few pounds of draw weight but had not expected anything like this.

Could the bison horn have added that much strength to the bow? It was time for a second opinion.

I took the bow to the local archery shop to measure the poundage on its bow scale. The employee manning the shop looked at me as if I was crazy when I told him I thought the bow was ninety pounds. I placed the bow on the scale and pushed down until I got the bow to twenty-three inches. The scale read eighty-two pounds. Holy cow, eighty-two pounds! The archery shop employee looked just as amazed as I was. Neither of us could believe what the scale was reading.

I thanked him and left. I knew I could not shoot a bow of eighty-two pounds comfortably. My hunting bow is only fifty-seven pounds. I was truly overbowed with this new one. I also realized there was more to this bow with a buffalo horn belly than I had originally thought, and I decided right then and there that I needed to make another one.

Again, I ordered buffalo horn caps. While I waited for them to arrive, I made another Osage orange bow with the exact same dimensions but with only twenty-five pounds of draw weight instead of forty. After a few days, the horn caps arrived, and again, I was eager to get in the shop and start to work. I followed my previous methods of construction and patiently waited for the bow to dry so I could test it.

When the day finally came to brace the bow, I managed to do it without straining myself. I did notice right off, however, that the lower limb was out of tiller. I had not planned on that happening. The only way the tiller could be adjusted was to scrape the horn belly. The problem was that I had all my sinew wraps in place and would have to be removed several before I could begin to scrape. I managed to remove the wraps and scrape the horn belly where the tiller needed to be adjusted. Truthfully, I was afraid to brace the bow for fear one of the horn pieces might pop loose.

I decided to wrap the joints with Dacron B-50 bowstring as tight as I could before bracing the bow. That temporary fix allowed me to brace the bow without any horn pieces coming loose. Then I adjusted the tiller accordingly. When the tiller was right, I replaced the sinew wrappings I had removed and allowed them to dry for several days.

When I braced the bow again, it was much smoother to draw, and it turned out to pull a little more than fifty pounds. That made me realize the horn can actually double the draw weight of a bow. I continued to shoot the bow for several weeks to test durability. The bow held up just fine and shot well. However, with Osage orange being such a dense, heavy wood, the bow was also quite heavy in the hand. The horn added a lot of physical weight to the bow as well. And I have found that a bow that is physically heavy can lose some of its power and cast.

I continued to make bows with buffalo horn bellies and I ended up making a dozen in all. I tried various woods, including hickory, hackberry, and black walnut. My conclusion after the experiment was this: Buffalo horn added to the belly of a bow can increase the compression a great deal, whereas dense woods with good compression, such as Osage wood, do not need any more compression added to the belly to increase performance. Adding the horn will only hinder it. If, however, you have a wood that is somewhat weak and not extremely dense, the horn can add a great deal to how the bow performs.

The experiment had been a valuable learning process. In all the bows I made of this design, I had only one on which a piece of horn separated from a bow. The sinew wraps at the joints did hold the horn to the bow, but it lifted in the middle. For my repair, I heated some hide glue, filled a syringe with it, and then squirted the glue under the lifting piece of horn before clamping the horn back down with several C-clamps. I allowed the repair to dry for a week before removing the clamps. Many years later, the bow's owner still shoots the bow, and it has held up just fine.

Bow making is always an adventure and often a learning process. After all these years of making bows, I still learn something new each time.

The Warrior's Gallery

Bows

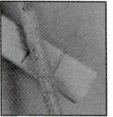

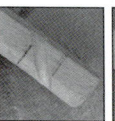

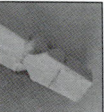

From left, making a bow nock to hold a bowstring.

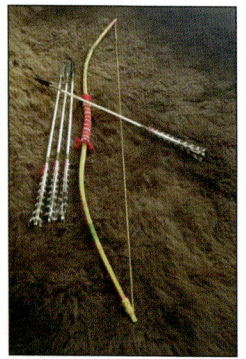

Clockwise from left, a bow with great tiller, a setback bow, a trade cloth handle bow, a recurved bow, and a sheep horn bow.

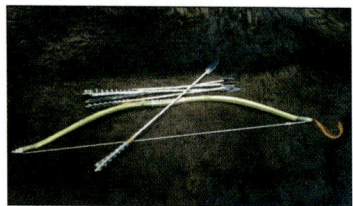

Arrows

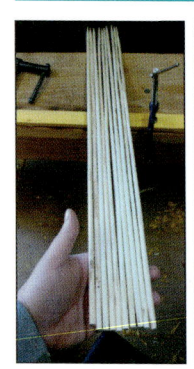

From left, dogwood shafts, nocked shafts pre-paint, nocked shafts painted, fletchings.

Above, rough arrowpoints. Left, arrowpoint insertion. Below, arrow blunts.

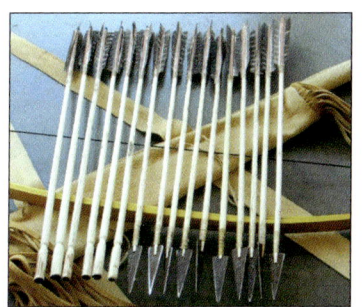

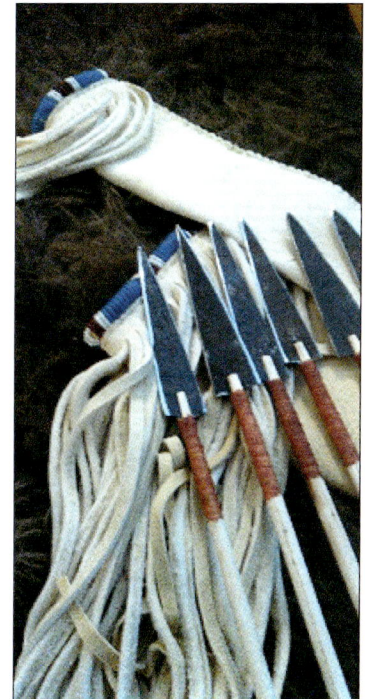

Above, finished arrowpoint details.

Quivers & Bow Cases

Above, my favorite quiver. Left, hanging quiver.

Above, a Strike a Light bag. Left, a kit.

Shields

Above, a Plains-style shield. Top left, a shield back. Bottom left, a shield cover.

Chapter 8
Shooting the Short Bow

OVER THE AGES, MANY a theory has surfaced when it comes to the shooting of the short bow. I wish I could say a secret theory existed that would ensure or improve accuracy, but in reality, the only surefire way to get better with the short bow is to practice shooting it—over and over.

Still, everyone swears by his own theory.

The key is to try all methods and find the one that works best for you. Most of the bows I make are between forty-four to forty-eight inches with draw lengths averaging twenty-two to twenty-four inches. Those are good average measurements of Plains bows, and the lengths work well with the following approaches.

The three things all shooting methods share is the need to cant the bow, to bend the bow arm outward at the elbow, and to use the push-pull method of drawing the bow.

Canting the bow is vitally important to the accuracy of a short bow. If you are holding the bow straight up and down in front of you representing noon on the clock, and then you want to hold the bow to about the two o'clock position to get the right angle of canting. If you are a lefty, it will be at the ten o'clock position. One of the reasons for this is that short bows are not drawn to the cheek as you would do with the common recurve or long bow, using a straight up-and-down body position and stiff bow arm, creating a straight line across the body at eye level. As a result, your line of sight is going to be different with a short bow.

By moving the bow to about the two o'clock position and not drawing toward your face with two of these methods, you remove the bow from your line of sight. That means you are not obstructing your vision of the target. It also eliminates some of the archer's paradox, and allows the arrow to pass from your hand (your hand being your arrow shelf) much more smoothly than if you had held the bow straight up and down.

The push-pull method involves pushing outward with your bow arm and pulling with your drawing hand at the same time. Usually, the bow will be raised slightly over the head and then pulled down toward the intended target. The method is incorporated to reach full draw. Once the full draw is reached, the arrow is loosed.

The push-pull method allows the archer to draw a heavier bow because he is using both arms to make the bow work instead of just one. As the bow is lowered into the shooting position, the target comes into view, allowing the archer to focus on the mark. A second later with the bow at full draw, the archer releases the arrow all in one fluid motion.

One of the methods used by the Plains tribes called for the archer to keep the bow arm outward and level with the shoulder but bent at the elbow outward and slightly angled downward. That leaves the shoulders a little more squared to the target as the string is drawn. Yet even with the arm toward the center of the chest, the archer is going to extend the thumb on the drawing hand outward until it touches the center of the chest. This point is the anchor, and the view the archer has looking down over the top of the arrow shaft instead of sighting down it.

Many archers are used to looking straight down their arrow at the target. That method forces the archer to focus on the target and takes the arrow as a sight out of the picture. It can take some getting used to, but once learned, it can be quite effective. It works well with bows of twenty-two-inch draw length or less. Using that particular method will increase your hand-to-eye coordination considerably.

Another method is drawing to the cheek or under the chin, but the body position is far different than what modern longbow and recurve shooters now use. The method causes the archer to bend the bow arm outward at the elbow, pushing the shoulders and neck forward, and drawing the bow to the cheek or under the chin—think of watching an adult pulling a child's compound bow to the cheek. The position necessary to manipulate the body and arm in to draw the bow to the cheek is just about the same method used when using a short bow.

Although I have seen the method used at some of our archery shoots, it still looks funny and unorthodox to me. However, for those used to having an anchor point on their face, it might be the best method to try. Just remember that you have to push your upper body forward and extend your chin outward to meet your drawing hand.

One friend of mine uses this method, and his draw is slightly shorter than he can push his chin forward, so he cannot quite get his hand to his chin. Instead, he extends his lips outward the half inch or so to reach his anchor point. It's quite amusing, to say the least, but I have to admit he has mastered his take on the method and is a real tough competitor.

Drawing the bow to your armpit while standing more sideways is another method. With this method, the body should be leaning forward at the hips, the bow canted, and the string drawn right in line with the armpit. Anchor is reached when the drawing hand touches the pectoral muscle. I like this method the best, and it is the one that works well for me out to twenty yards. I like standing sideways when shooting a short bow with my bow arm pointing right toward my target and my feet a little less than shoulder width apart. I replicate the same method when on horseback, although I have to admit the sight picture does change when I am galloping on the back of a horse.

The floating anchor method is the last one I am going to discuss. Having an anchor point is very important when it comes to archery. If you draw your bow back to the same spot every time —and assuming you are doing everything else right, such as grip, release, and sight picture—in theory, your bow should shoot the same every time. Vice versa, if you are not drawing the bow the same way and same distance every time, you will have sporadic arrow placement, to say the least. The floating anchor is hard to master but without a doubt has been used for centuries.

The method is simple. It is basically any one of the aforementioned methods—but without touching any anchor point. The archer simply draws the bow and lets the arrow loose without coming to an anchor stopping point before release. The only way I can figure that the archer knows when to stop drawing is if the arrows were cut to the exact length needed for the bow to be at full draw. From my research over the years, I think most Plains bows had arrows that were matched to the bow just like archers of today, and they drew their arrows to the head just as we do.

After talking with elders and reading historical accounts, it is my belief that the Plains Indians were snap shooters. What I mean by that is that once full draw was achieved, they released the arrow.

They did not hold at full draw as many modern shooters do. It is also worth mentioning that among Plains tribes, the three-finger bow release we use, often called the Mediterranean release, was almost unheard of back then. The Plains tribes used a pinch grip or an augmented pinch grip when shooting their bows. It calls for pinching the bowstring and arrow between the thumb and index finger. The second and third fingers are added to the bowstring only if needed. I have tried the method and cannot come close to drawing an arrow back with it. Having grown up using the three-finger method, I find the pinch grip foreign.

In paintings of the Plains tribes, Indians are often seen holding their bows perfectly straight up and down in what I call a modern bow stance. Their bows are drawn to their cheeks, with their quivers draped across their backs in the same way quivers are worn today, and the archers are depicted drawing arrows over their shoulders from the quivers. That is not an accurate depiction of the Plains warrior using a bow and quiver.

Although some painters got it right, showing canted bows and bows being drawn to the chest rather than to the cheek or to eye level, many paintings are plain wrong. The pictures were painted in the way the painter understood archery, which was mostly the European style, rather than how they witnessed it in use by Indians. Early drawings of Cherokees erroneously showed them having recurved bows with horn nocks. Such bows were strictly European bows, not Cherokee.

History has left us with many such mysteries. Because none of us was alive when the tribes were chasing down buffalo on horseback, we are left with only the rare description of those hunts, the misrepresented paintings of early frontier painters, or the stories of tribal elders. I think when you look at old accounts and add that to the stories of tribal elders who still have knowledge of the subject, then apply practical application, you can see that all the methods addressed here do work. Regardless, you will have fun trying them.

In the beginning, it is always good to practice at a short distance. I usually start by shooting at ten yards. When I can get five or six arrows in a paper plate at that distance, I move to fifteen yards and then to twenty. Twenty-five yards is my limited range with a short bow. I really have to practice to keep all my arrows in a fifteen-inch grouping. That could well be because the bows were meant for close and personal use, although I have no doubt, given written accounts, that Plains Indians could easily use the short bow effectively to sixty yards.

The bows can shoot much greater distances than that, but arrows were rarely wasted on shots that would not end in results. Still, it has been reported on more than one occasion that arrows were lobbed in a general direction of an enemy with great effect and accuracy. It always takes me twice as long to make a nice set of six dogwood arrows as it does a nice self bow. So I understand not wanting to make a wasted shot and possibly losing an arrow.

The rate of fire from an accomplished Plains archer is something that many frontiersmen, soldiers, and other firsthand witnesses have commented on throughout the years. It was often said a mounted Plains warrior could get an arrow in the air and five more would be en route before the first one hit. I have personally tried to reproduce this on several occasions—launching an arrow upward at a safe angle and trying to get several more in the air before the first one came down. I am sad to say that I have managed to get only two arrows in the air before the first one hit the ground, and I am known for shooting very fast in timed events. It would take a master archer indeed to rapid-fire arrows in the manner attributed to the Plains warriors.

That reminds me of a story from my own family history. Because I am Chickasaw and Irish/Black Dutch, I have interesting

The Warrior's Tools

history on both sides of the family. On my nonnative side, my maternal great-great-grandfather, Joseph Austin Dennis, on the latter side, owned land in the Bulcher–Saint Jo area in north Texas in the mid- to late 1800s. By all accounts, he was a rough and tough man but also well educated and soft spoken. As with most people of the day, he owned livestock, including a great many horses. Family history has it that he traded horses with the Jesse James gang. One night, he even supposedly offered to let the outlaws sleep in his barn. They are said to have declined because they did not want to bring harm to the family in case they were being followed, and so they continued on to the creek to camp instead. But that's a story for another day.

Over the years, Joseph had many interesting encounters, including with Comanches. Comanches, as with all Plains tribes, considered horse stealing to be both a virtuous and brave act; it was one of many traits that made a man well respected among his fellow tribesmen. By that time, the Comanches were already on the reservation set aside for them at Fort Sill, Indian Territory, now modern Oklahoma, and on that day, several Comanches had left the reservation and gone to Texas to steal horses. They ended up taking some of Joseph's herd before hightailing it back north to Fort Sill.

However, before the renegades could cross the Red River, the boundary between Texas and Indian Territory, Joseph and his brother were not only on their trail but had caught up with them. As the fight ensued, the Comanches broke off in different directions still pushing the stolen horses in front of them. One of the warriors, distinctive in a black cowboy hat, stayed on course and launched arrows at the pursuers from horseback. He was serving as a rearguard to allow his companions to escape with the horses.

They reached the river, and the final lone Comanche hid in a thicket on the far side, with Joseph and his brother on the near side. At this point of the story, Joseph always noted that from a distance of three hundred feet, a Comanche could hit you with an arrow if you stood still, but since you could see the arrow coming, you had time to get out of the way. The only catch: You had to watch for the other three or four arrows that would be following the first.

Joseph's brother was a crack shot, and from across the river, he could just make out a black hat in the thicket. He aimed at the hat and squeezed off a round. Certain that he had hit his mark, the brothers crossed the river and headed into the thicket where the Comanche had last been spotted. All they found was the tassel of a hatband, sheared clean off by the round that had been fired.

There was no sign of the Comanche.

When I think about this old family story, I always assume the Comanche, wanting to keep his head and having only a bow against two guns, decided the better part of valor was to flee and live to fight another day. I don't blame him.

I never knew whether Joseph got his horses back because the story always seemed to end with the empty thicket. That's how my grandfather relayed it to me, anyway. I suppose it was a cautionary tale of sorts, with the point being, once more, that a Comanche can get several arrows in the air before the first one hits the ground, but he can also hit his target on horseback. That is real testament to the power and accuracy of a Plains bow in the hands of a skilled archer.

Nowadays, such bows—and most all bows made of natural materials—are called *primitive*. A decade ago, the term was *traditional*. Now the modern glass-backed recurve and longbows are *traditional*, and any wood or composite bow is *primitive*.

That last term always reminds me of a caveman carrying around a club. It is also way off the mark. There is nothing primitive about the Plains Indian bow at all. Complex in design and function, it takes great skill to make and use, and it can kill any animal in North America. It was the main weapon of choice on the frontier for Indians even after black powder guns and single-shot rifles came onto the scene. The Plains bow was only outgunned, so to speak, only when the six-shot revolver was developed. That gun tipped the odds in the favor of those who had such weapons and changed the face of warfare on the Great Plains.

One of the advantages I find with a short bow is its ease of maneuverability, which means you can easily carry the bow through the woods and shoot while standing or kneeling. Doing either of those, you will rarely hang the bow up on limbs or brush. The short bow is easy to use off horseback too, and it can be concealed easily under a buffalo robe, along with a handful of arrows if necessary.

I have been asked several times about one particular aspect of the many historic photographs of Native warriors riding horseback or standing for a studio portrait while holding a bow in one hand and a handful of arrows in the other—with arrow tips pointing upward. The reason behind that posture is simple and sensible. If you have ever tried horseback archery of any form, you know even the most experienced archer will occasionally hit the horse or his own legs, especially the thighs, with the bottom limb of the bow. And if you have a handful of arrows with razor-sharp points in your hand, you would not want yourself or the horse to get all cut up. It only makes sense to hold the arrows with the points pointing upward rather than downward. Another reason for carrying a few arrows in your hand is nothing less than having another arrow readily available for the next shot.

Plains bows did not come with arrow shelves or rests. Some had buckskin or cloth wrapped around the handle, but all the bows were shot off the hand, meaning the hand was the arrow shelf. Some of the wider bows of the historic Plains had a narrower handle section to help reduce some of the archer's paradox. I have even seen a few bows tillered to the side to help the string align more to the side on which the arrow was shot. No doubt this was to help in a smoother arrow pass.

Of the many Plains Indian bow designs, I have found no bow easier to shoot than the D-shaped, bend-through-the-handle bow. Such a bow is easy to brace, smooth to shoot, and forgiving, unlike the heavy reflexed bows or bow with setback handles that kick in the handle and can be a real pain to string without twisting in your hand.

The D-shaped bow is also the easiest to make, simple yet effective. The ideal D-shaped bow is fifty inches long tip to tip and forty-eight-and-a-half inches from nock to nock with a one-inch-wide handle section. It is one-and-a-half inches to one-and-three-quarters inches wide at the midlimbs tapering to three-quarters inches at the tips. I always leave an extra inch of wood at the end so I can carve out a small protruding tip to which to attach some horsehair.

I like the bow to draw between forty-five to fifty pounds at twenty-four inches of draw length. You can play around with bow and draw length until you find the right combination for you, but remember, if you use the push-pull method of drawing, in a very short time, you can draw a bow of heavier poundage. I even use the push-pull method of drawing when I shoot my longer bows; it has always worked well for me.

I am not limited to a fifty-pound bow, and I own bows much heavier than that, but a bow of fifty-pound draw weight is something I can easily shoot all day. To achieve accuracy with any bow, you need to draw the bow with ease and not struggle. That will result in fewer mistakes and teach you how to shoot the bow without the distraction of fighting with heavy draw weight.

Chapter 9
Plains Indian Arrows

THERE IS NOTHING MORE beautiful than a set of handmade arrows to complement your bow. However, I should warn you now that arrows are difficult to make, and they take more time, patience, and skill than making a self bow.

Arrow woods varied among the Plains tribes, but dogwood, serviceberry, chokecherry, and red willow were commonly used. I have seen a few Plains arrows made of river cane as well, although it was used more by tribes in various parts of the country east and west of the Great Plains.

The common Plains arrow had elongated feathers, some as long as eight inches in length. Three feathers were the standard, but occasionally you would see an arrow fletched, or feathered, with only two. The feathers were usually trimmed low to the shaft and often glued into place with hide glue.

Some Plains arrows were not glued but rather tied in such a way that the feathers would lie along the shaft nice and secure.

All the arrows were secured at the top and bottom of the fletchings with fine pieces of sinew that usually had been dipped in hot hide glue and then allowed to dry. It made for a smooth wrap that would hold the feathers in place for a long time.

When I fletch my arrows, I use modern Super Glue instead of hide glue for its fast bonding time. It is both inexpensive and works well. I have tried the gel-type Super Glue, but it does not hold as well as the liquid Super Glue. However, I still use hide glue to do my sinew work.

Historically, arrows with decorations tied into the base of the fletchings were common. The decorations might be tufts of horsehair, yarn, bird down, or the tip of the feather itself, which when cut to size and left untrimmed made a little tail at the base of each feather. Fletchings varied greatly, and in many cases, raptor feathers were used. It was common to see the use of feathers from the red-tailed hawk, the preferred fletching of the Comanches, along with eagle, prairie falcon, and owl. Turkey and buzzard feathers were also used. Today, all those birds are protected by federal game laws, and using feathers from any of them would bring serious charges, with the exception of turkey. Turkey feathers can be purchased on websites for hide and fur, crafts, or mountain-man products. Turkey featheres are great for fletching and were commonly used by the Cheyenne. I should note that the wing and secondary feathers are preferred to the tail, which is not as durable or stiff.

It can be challenging to try to determine arrow origins because of the similar styles of Plains tribes. Arrows were a popular commodity item and were used in all forms of barter and trade. Arrows that were captured from enemies, picked up after battles, or won by gambling were considered a real prize.

Although you can see distinguishing traits among some tribal arrows such as nock design, fletching styles, markings, and length of arrowpoints, it is not as easy to determine what came from where by looking at random arrows displayed in museums or featured in photographs or books. Quite often, you see variations even among arrow makers of the same tribe, causing official identification of old arrows to be difficult. Unless the arrow was documented when collected and was known to be collected from a certain tribe, you would be hard pressed to know its origins in most cases.

Comanche arrows were usually the one exception because of the unique way Comanches fletched their arrows. Comanche feathers were tied down with a protruding piece of quill left on the end of the feather at the nock, pointing in the opposite direction of the shaft, and then folded back over and secured. Comanche arrow makers often then added a fine piece of sinew and wrapped it through the top of the fletching another inch, ensuring a good secure fletch. The arrows were often fletched without glue, but the Comanche's method ensured that the fletching would stay in place. The Comanche arrows also rarely had as long a fletching as the ones from tribes north of them, and, in general, Comanche arrowpoints were wider and shorter than arrows from other tribes on the Northern Plains.

There is much speculation about the reasons behind the Plains Indians' use of elongated fletching. After much study, I have concluded that with a heavy shaft in high prairie winds, the low-cut feathers slice through the air exceptionally well, and the length helps to stabilize the shaft. A shorter, wider fletch would have been more likely to veer off course, catching the wind in flight.

Many Southern Plains arrows, just like all arrows of the Plains tribes, were grooved along the shaft with straight, wavy, or zigzag patterns or any combination of the three. Some arrows from all of the Plains tribes could also be found without any shaft grooves, but grooves were used more often than not.

I have heard over and over from Sioux people that the zigzag pattern grooved into the shaft represented lightning bolts, and it was put there to invoke the speed of lightning. That might well be the symbolism of the design, but the fact remains that such grooves also helped to keep the shafts straight. I have also heard that the grooves allowed the blood to flow more easily from the wound made by such an arrow. That is rubbish!

Arrows of the Plains were usually fletched without any helical, or spiral. That means the feathers were laid down straight on the shaft without any twist. Even when fletched in that manner, an arrow would retain some spin in flight. Arrowpoints were attached usually in one of two ways. They were either in line with the cock feather, making the point horizontal at full draw, or they were opposite the cock feather, making the point vertical at full draw. Both methods work in the same way.

Many writers have said arrows were usually attached to be vertical at full draw when hunting buffalo so the arrowhead would be in the same position as the ribs of the buffalo, allowing the arrow to enter the rib cage much easily. Because an arrow will spin to some degree no matter how it is fletched, I do not believe this line of thinking has any merit.

Arrowheads were attached the same way on most arrows, with either a groove or notch cut into the end of the shaft long enough for the base of the point to fit securely. I believe hide glue was then inserted into the groove and smeared on the shank of the point before its insertion. Then sinew was wrapped for extra security. On some arrows, the sinew on the base of the point was wrapped up the shaft for several inches. I believe this extra reinforcement was to help the shaft stay intact if the arrow hit a bone.

Many shafts were decorated with dye made from plants or rocks with mineral properties that gave color. As in modern times, cresting was used in a variety of colors. Each archer usually had his own cresting to ensure that no mistakes were made when an animal was harvested. It is said that if a buffalo had been shot by more than one hunter, the man who drew first blood usually claimed the meat. However, he would generally share a portion of it with the hunter who had helped to finish off the animal.

Throughout the Plains, arrow material was collected in winter when tree sap was low. It was the only time the Indians could collect material to make successful arrows, unless they were using river cane. River cane was harvested in the summer when it was green, and it was allowed to dry. Arrow-shaft materials were collected while the sap was low because otherwise, the shaft would crack as it dried, making for a less than suitable arrow. Arrows were collected and trimmed to a little longer than the desired length and usually wrapped in bundles with rawhide.

When I collect dogwood shafts, I remove the bark from the shaft, or rod, of wood, and then bundle the shafts together to dry. I try to cut shafting about the size of my thumb and bundle the shafts by quality. The fewer knots there are on a wood shaft, the easier it is to work, although I must say that all-natural shafting will have some knots.

Once I have the shafts peeled of bark, I straighten them by hand, sighting down the shaft and bending where needed. You will repeat this many times, but at this stage, the shafts are usually easy to bend. I then wrap the bundles with cordage or zip ties and set them aside to cure. I have found that removing the bark makes the shafts dry much faster, and bundling them prestraightened will allow them to dry in that position.

After a week of drying, the bundles will become loose and have to be retied. If zip ties were used, you will have to pull them tighter. As the shafts lose moisture, they shrink and harden. You can speed up the drying process by using a heat gun and getting the shafts very hot. You will need to do this several times to get all the moisture out of the wood. The Plains tribes usually heated their shafts over hot coals or put them next to a fire, rotating the shafts occasionally to dry them out. I have read of shafts being greased and heated to straighten. I have never cut a shaft so poor in quality that I had to use grease to work out a kink. With such a huge selection of wild shafting around, it is wiser to just take the extra time to collect shafts that are as straight as possible. Besides, glue does not stick well to grease.

When heating dogwood, willow, serviceberry, and chokecherry, you will notice that a lot of shafts tend to warp. Do not panic. That is normal. When the shaft is cool enough to handle, straighten it, and go on to the next.

Larger shafts can sometimes be hard to straighten by hand. A simple jig can be made to aid in the process. My jig is an old piece of an Osage orange bow limb about six inches long that I have drilled holes into toward one end. One hole is a half inch, and the other is an inch. You can slide the shaft into the hole and use it to give you extra leverage in bending the shaft straight, simply by applying pressure in the opposite direction. It should be noted that shafts are easier to bend when hot. If you find a stubborn section, heat that section with a heat gun or over the stove and then begin the straightening process.

I used to work all my arrows with a wood file first, somewhat squaring the shaft with the file and then rounding off the square edges. I would scrape excess material off the shaft with a square-edged knife blade until the arrow looked and felt right in my hand. It took a long time. At one point, I was getting so many orders for arrows that I had to find another way. After much trial and error with dowel cutters and block planes, I finally turned to my six-inch by forty-eight-inch belt sander.

It proved to be a revelation. If I held the shaft flat on the sander with my left hand and spun the shaft back and forth with my right, as the belt removed material, I could quickly get a worked-down shaft in mere minutes. It took a while to get the hang of it, but once perfected, it saved me hours of handwork. My first arrows came out oblong with waves and divots, but once I learned how to apply pressure at the right place as I worked the shaft, the arrows started to take shape. After that, I never looked back. Yes, you still have to get the final size by scraping and sanding, but with a little practice, this method will produce nice shafting in no time.

My experience with making shafts using a belt sander also brought me to the conclusion that if you cut a thicker diameter shaf, you can eliminate flaws much more easily. There is more wood to remove, but in the end, you get better quality shafts. The sander automatically takes off any high spots, and by spinning the shaft as you go, you can quickly make a large round shaft thinner.

If you choose to leave the bark on your arrow shafts and let them dry longer, you can work the shafts on the sander with the bark on as long as the shaft is dry. A green shaft will gum up a sanding belt in a matter of seconds and cause a lot of unnecessary frustration. The shafting will need to be straight before trying to use the sander; otherwise, you will not succeed.

It is worth mentioning here that I use the bottom end, or the end that I cut closest to the ground, as the nock end. I have always done this, and usually I add a little more weight toward the front of the shaft with a heavy point to counteract the long fletchings. I have read that is the opposite way the Plains tribes supposedly did it, but after making thousands of dogwood arrows, this method works well for me. As a result, I have made some excellent shooting arrows. Either way will work. It just comes down to personal preference.

Back in the day, archers did not have the luxury of belt sanders, and so they found a variety of ways to work down arrow shafts. I am sure one method was to peel away the wood with a knife until a roughed-out shape was obtained and then to use a set of sandstone blocks. The blocks would have varied in length, but most would have fit in the palm of the hand. The center was grooved out in a semicircular groove. The arrow would be laid in the groove, and the other block was put on top. The arrow maker then pushed and pulled the arrow back and forth the entire length of the shaft until the arrow shaft was worked to size.

After the shafts are finished, you need to groove them.

I use two grooves. One is on the opposite side of the shaft from where the base of the fletching is going to be, and the other is on the point of the arrow.

There are many methods to apply these grooves, but before we get into that, let me explain the reason for them. All wood retains and releases moistures with the seasons. That is true of bows as well. Even a fine well oiled self bow will gain some moisture in the cold and wet seasons and release it in the hot and dry seasons. This change can be noticed when you shoot the bow in different temperatures. When I shoot my favorite Osage wood self bow in winter, it always seems a little sluggish, whereas in the summer, the string almost hums when an arrow is loosed. The reason is the moisture content of the wood.

Unless you have a lacquer, polyurethane, or several coats of True oil on your bow, it more than likely reacts to moisture in the same way. Being a traditionalist to some degree, I only oil my bows. I do not seal them as most modern bowyers do, so the seasonal changes are something I am used to.

The grooves cut into the arrow shafts allow moisture to be released from the shaft pretty much its entire length, thus helping to keep the shaft straight. Notice I said "helping." You will still have to occasionally straighten the shafts by hand. By then, it usually won't require any heat unless you have an unruly shaft.

The grooves in an arrow can be applied with a simple jig. To make a jig, take a small piece of wood two inches by four-and-a-half inches and drill a hole somewhat larger than the diameter of the shaft. If the shafts average five-sixteenths inch in diameter, drill the hole eleven-and-thirty-seconds inch. Hammer a small finishing nail into the top of the wood so that the nail protrudes just enough through the hole to cut a groove in the shaft. Insert the shaft into the hole and cut your groove.

You can start out with a straight groove. Once you have the jig set up accordingly, practice the zigzag pattern. Do not just scratch the surface of the shaft with the nail; instead, make sure you cut deep enough to go through the outer layer of wood. You can mark on the shaft with a pencil where the feathers will go. I usually stop at that point, but I should note that many Plains arrows were grooved the entire length of the shaft.

Indians used a similar method of grooving their shafts by using an antler with a hole that had been bored through, leaving a small piece of antler protruding through the hole. The protrusion cut the groove into the shaft. I have read they also used a knife to make the shaft grooves, but having actually tried it, I found it not to be a proficient way of doing it.

I cut the groove for the point and the nock. That can be done by taping two hacksaw blades together. The width of the two blades is the ideal size for points made of barrel-hoop iron. If you have a Dremel power tool with a cutting wheel, it will work as well—just be sure to wear eye protection.

After cutting the desired nock shape, take the time to smooth it out with sandpaper so no burrs remain in the nock groove that could damage the bowstring. Nocks can be made to whatever desired shape you like. They should always be reinforced with sinew so that they do not split when the arrow is released. No one wants shards of wood shooting off in unknown directions—such as toward your wrist.

The traditional method of doing this same thing was usually with a knife that had been turned into a saw with the blade thin enough to make a groove the desired width for inserting the point. In those days, many knives were altered to become saws simply by chipping the blade in alternating sections to make a sawlike blade. Such a knife also worked for making the nocks.

After you have finished the the point and nocks, give the shaft a good once-over with fine sandpaper until it is smooth to the touch. Indians used heavy leather for the first sanding and then a piece of antler to burnish the shaft to a shine. To burnish, you can use any smooth material harder than the shaft. A piece of copper tubing works well, but then so does a deer or elk tine. I would not suggest burnishing the shafts where you intend to crest them, because once burnished, the wood will have hardened and compressed, and your color will have a hard time soaking in.

Premade metal points, sheets of iron, and various other metalwares were traded to the tribes for buffalo robes, beaver, and other furs the Indians had harvested. When no trade points were at hand, Indians made them from the bottom of metal frying pans or the iron bands used on wooden barrels, sometimes called "hoop iron," as well as any other materials that they could get ahold of that would make a suitable point.

I have read that Indians also used the iron bands from around the outside of a wagon wheel to make arrowheads. Having seen many of those old rings, I think that would be an almost impossible task because that iron was thick and heavy. Even if a point could be cut from the thick iron with a rudimentary saw, the points would be extremely heavy.

I make points from old iron barrel rings. Occasionally you can find antique barrels for sale, but new ones are also still being produced, and they are the ideal thickness. The iron is soft and thus fairly easy to cut with simple tools to make good usable points.

The easiest way I have found to cut such points is to first cut out a section seven inches long. A strip of that length should yield six arrowpoints three inches long with a half-inch shank. Next, I draw out my pattern with a silver marker and cut the points with a sharp pair of metal shears. After cutting, the iron will curl and not be straight, so it will be necessary to lay the points on a hard surface and use a hammer to pound them back flat.

A simple benchtop grinder will work for the initial edge. Then a round chainsaw file can be used to put the final hunting edge on the points. A Dremel power tool with a cutting wheel can be used to cut grooves in the shank if you like to give the sinew wrapping something to bind to when the points are attached to the shaft. Safety glasses are a must when doing this.

Indians of old used various rocks to sharpen points. In later years, they traded for files and used them. An iron point will bend if impacted on a hard surface such as a rib bone, but the point can be hammered straight again and used over and over. Bone and antler were often used for effective points.

Bone and antler can also be worked down to a fine edge hard enough to penetrate flesh. The method of attaching a point of that type is the same as used when attaching a metal one. There is so much information available about flint arrowheads that I will only add my personal thoughts on the subject here. Flint and stone arrowheads were used all the way through the Plains horse culture period, but they were not preferred over points of metal when metal was at hand.

If you decide to try river cane for arrow shafting, there are many good ways to go about it. river cane is nothing more than bamboo, and bamboo makes excellent arrows. You could almost compare the fibrous content of a river cane shaft to a modern-day carbon arrow.

River cane grows in sections, with a nodule found at each new section and so on. Each section is a little thinner in diameter than the one before it. As I mentioned before, river cane should be cut green and then allowed ample time to dry. I lay mine outside on my daughter's trampoline, where the shafts can get plenty of sun from above and ventilation from below.

After the shafts are dry, they will need to be straightened. I use a heat gun for that job. River cane is easier to straighten than wood shafting. I scrape the shaft clean with my pocketknife and sand each nodule down until it is smooth. Then I use the heat gun, heating only the spots that need to be straightened. Be careful not to overheat the shaft. Like wood, bamboo is flammable.

Usually you can get river-cane shafts good and straight by heating only the nodules. When a nodule is heated and bent, it bends the whole section of the shaft in front of it. So start with the first nodule on the cane and work your way down the shaft nodule by nodule. The thinner end of the shaft will always be the nock end, and the larger end will be the point end.

River cane does not work the same as wood.

If you try to taper an end, you will end up tapering and tapering some more, and then some more, until eventually you have cut several inches off the shaft. Instead, remove some of the pith from the already hollowed-out cane shaft—just enough to insert a worked-down piece of hardwood for a foreshaft, basically the forward portion of the arrow shaft. The pieces need to fit snug. Once you have made a snug fit for the foreshaft, it can be glued into place with hide glue or wood glue and allowed to dry.

You will need to sand where you paired the two pieces of wood to ensure that they are flush and then wrap them with sinew dipped in hot hide glue. With the sinew dry, you have a secure shaft. You can attach the point to the foreshaft, as mentioned earlier. I like to already have my points attached to the foreshaft before I do the final glue-up.

River cane needs no hardwood nock, but the nock does need to be reinforced well with sinew. I reinforce my cane arrows with a half-inch section of sinew and have never had a nock separate. If you want to get fancy, you can use the same method, as we just discussed, to add a nock of hardwood, bone, antler, or horn.

Cane arrows do not hold paint well, so I usually add horsehair to the base of the fletchings to add a little flair. I also like to paint the sinew bindings a brilliant color. It adds a nice detail to the cane arrows and makes them stand out.

Although it is much easier to order a dozen arrows and have them delivered to your front door than it is harvest the material and make your own, I take a great deal of satisfaction in shooting arrows that I have made from a bow I have made. Every time I harvest an animal with my tackle, I feel a connection with people of the past. Yes, I could go to the store and buy meat, which I do most months of the year, but to do it the hard way and the way our ancestors did results in an amazing feeling of accomplishment and satisfaction that cannot easily be described.

I always tell my students that archery is the common bond among people of all nations, with few exceptions. At some time in all of our people's history, we used the bow and arrow. Although our languages, our customs, our skin colors, our songs and dances might be different, we all have archery in common.

Chapter 10

Plains Indian Quivers

PLAINS INDIAN QUIVERS ARE as beautiful as they are functional. Many were adorned with beadwork, quillwork, brightly colored trade cloth, feathers, bells, and handmade tin cones, and their decoration varied from tribe to tribe.

The overall design of the bow case and quiver, however, were similar. The quiver holds the arrows. The bow case is a sleeve attached to the quiver that a bow slides into. When someone refers to a Plains Indian quiver, I usually take it to mean they are talking about the bow case and quiver as one rig because the bow case was usually present on Plains quivers. So when I refer to a Plains quiver, I am talking about the quiver with an attached bow case.

Quivers were made from various tanned animal hides, with whitetail, mule deer, and elk hides having the ideal thickness. I have found antelope buckskin to be too thin for a good durable quiver, and buffalo hide is generally far too thick for my preference, although buffalo was often used. A prized quiver could also have been made from a bobcat or mountain-lion pelt. However, because those animals are protected in some states, I have never made a quiver from either.

The women of the tribe tanned hides, and it fell to them to make the hides soft and pliable with the use of different mixtures of organs and the brain of the animal. Such hides are known today as brain tanned. Most hides were then smoked, allowing the hide, if wet, to be softened back again and to keep it from becoming hard or plagued by dry rot as commercial chemically tanned hides are today. Brain-tanned hides will lasts virtually a lifetime.

The quiver itself was made long enough for the arrows to be sufficiently deep enough inside it to keep the feathers covered. Generally, a stiffening rod was inserted into the inside of the quiver along the top seam. It was either sewed or tied into place with buckskin thongs. The rod was made from various woods, but a raw arrow shaft works just as well. Both of them allow the quiver to keep its overall shape when all the arrows are removed. In some quivers, the rod protrudes several inches beyond the end of the quiver, and it might be beaded or have a horsehair tassel attached for decoration.

Many quivers had what was called an arrow cup, a piece of rawhide or stiff leather sewed together to form a small cup or bowl. The cup was attached to the bottom of a long slender stick with rawhide, buckskin, or sinew. It could then be slid into the quiver with the cup at the bottom. The end of the stick would protrude several inches from the mouth of the quiver. The arrows were then slid into the quiver with the points inside the arrow cup. When the stick was pulled out, it raised all the arrows up out of the quiver for the archer to have easy access for shooting. The arrow cup was used across the plains.

Many Plains quivers were highly decorated to show the prestige or wealth of the owner. Just like the clothing people wore, decoration varied, but a man who was well off conveyed that by wearing heavily beaded clothing and adornments. Fur traders and trappers from Canada brought in beads, so at first, beads were easier to obtain in the Northern Plains than farther south.

In the south, the Comanche often showed wealth or prestige by the amount of fine double-rolled buckskin fringe they had on their shirts, moccasins, and leggings. The unique fringes were also seen on quivers of the era.

Green, yellow, and rust-colored ochre was used to beautify some clothing and adornments. Beadwork was done in smaller sections, usually consisting of only a few rows. On the Northern Plains, however, tribes would bead nice big panels on their shirts, leggings, moccasins, and quivers. It is now acceptable for men as well as women to do beadwork and quillwork, but it is my thinking that in that era, they were done mostly by women in the tribe.

The Plains quiver was worn across the lower back or to the side of the body, and it generally had the arrows protruding from the left side. If the archer was left-handed, then the arrows protruded from the right. When the quiver was in use, the bowyer would slide it around to the side or front of the body. Arrows were never drawn from a quiver by reaching over the shoulder, despite what the Europeans did or the movies suggest. If you were right-handed, you would naturally draw arrows with your right hand. So if the quiver rests on your back with arrows protruding to the left side and then is slid around to your front, the arrows are pointing to the right, making them easy to draw with your right hand.

Many frontier painters as well as modern ones get this wrong, painting arrows as being drawn over the shoulder. The way they show or depict the quiver is actually backward. If not, most Plains Indians were left-handed in the old days.

The side of the hide that would have held the hair of the animal is the outside of the quiver, with the underside forming the inside.

The outer layer of buckskin, or the hair side, is smoother and more appealing to look at when the hide is tanned. The underside tends to have a rough surface and is not as pleasing to the eye.

Each quiver was tailor-made to fit the owner unless a set had been captured in battle or obtained in a trade. Each man knew his draw length and favorite bow length, so quivers and bow cases were made to fit them. Again, it was standard for the bow to protrude several inches from the case and the arrows only an inch or so. The arrows were set deep in the quiver to protect them from the elements, basically to keep them dry. Quivers were made to hold ten to fifty arrows. It is widely believed that only ten arrows were carried when the archer was hunting, but when he was going to war, forty was the norm.

I asked Comanche elder Carney Saupitty how many arrows Comanches carried when hunting.

He replied, "Ten."

I asked him how many when going to war, and he replied, "Forty to fifty."

Of all the old quivers I have seen in museums, I have seen only a couple of them large enough to carry forty or fifty arrows. Most quivers look as though they would have a capacity of ten to fifteen arrows. It is my opinion that many men had more than one quiver. One was highly decorated for parading around camp and going to war. (Of course, you would want to impress your enemy as well as your fellow tribesmen.) And one was more basic and utilitarian. Basic quivers were made in the same way as the fancier ones but had fewer decorations.

I still find a plain buckskin quiver with nice fringe very appealing, and I make that kind quite often. They are virtually silent in the woods, and the rich smoked color of the hide blends in with nature. When it comes to my own quivers, I always use brain-tanned buckskin.

If you do not have a source for that, you can purchase quality-grade commercial deer or elk buckskin. Either of those will work fine. The hide, however, needs to be at least ten feet square to be large enough for the project.

Other supplies required include a carpenter's square, scissors, and pencil. When you outline the buckskin, place the smooth side down and the rough side facing up; all of your markings will be on the rough side. That is the side that will be on the inside of the quiver and will not be seen. I measure a fourteen-inch line on the center of the buckskin and mark the halfway point at seven inches.

Next, I line the square up on the seven-inch mark and draw a straight line down twenty-four inches. At the twenty-four-inch mark, make another line twelve inches long or six inches on either side of the bottom-center mark. Then line up the edges of the bottom line with the top line using the square, and connect them with the pencil on both sides. You now have the quiver drawn out.

The center of the hide is used because it has the most even thickness and is usually the best part of the hide. Your quiver has the most visible surface area so you want to use the best part of the hide for that section.

The bow case will be forty inches long by five-and-a-half-inches wide, basically the measurement for a forty-four-inch bow. If you are making a bow longer than that, the bow case should be four inches shorter than the bow, so adjust accordingly. The strap should be cut into two sections measuring thirty-six inches long by one-and-a-half inches wide.

Sew the two pieces together to make a six-inch strap. Now cut the sections that will be used for fringe. For the mouth of the quiver, you will need one section fourteen-and-a-half inches by ten inches. The bottom of the quiver will require a piece that measures twelve-and-a-half inches by ten inches. You will also need one section that measures five-and-three-quarter inches by six inches for the mouth of the bow case. Last, for the bottom of the case, you need another section of hide five-and-three-quarter inches by six-inches.

I like to cut all the fringe a half inch wider than what it is fitting around to make sure I do not come up short. If you have a little extra, just trim it off with scissors. Before you cut the pieces, mark the fringes so you will know where each one goes. On all the fringe pieces, measure half an inch down from the top, and draw a line across from one side to the other. Mark each piece accordingly, labeling the fringe that will go around the mouth of the quiver "QM" for "quiver mouth" and "QB" for the "quiver bottom."

Mark the other two fringe pieces accordingly. One tip: Use the same dimensions for all the pieces, and you can't go wrong. It will ensure that there is no mix-up when the time comes to sew everything together. With everything marked, it is time to cut.

Your scissors should be sharp, and you should be careful to stay on the lines you drew. Once the pieces are all cut, do the fringe. Cut each piece up to the half-inch line you drew earlier. The attention to detail will make all the fringe even, and it will look nice when attached to the quiver. In my opinion, thinner fringes look better than wide ones, so cut your fringe nice and thin.

I like to sew my quivers with backstrap sinew, but artificial sinew works well too, and it can be split down to workable widths. In my experience, a glovers' needle will work better than a regular sewing needle. When using a visible stitch, a whipstitch is the most appealing.

The fringe on the mouth of the quiver and the mouth of the bow case should be laid so that the top part of the fringe meets with the top part of the quiver and bow case, where it will lie flush. The bottom fringe will be attached to the bottom of the bow case, and the bottom of the quiver will be laid half an inch above the bottom.

If you try to sew the fringe in place after you sew up the quiver, you will find some problems when it comes to getting things even, especially on the bottom. That can be avoided by putting a layer of wood glue on the underside of the fringe right along the top edge and gluing the fringe into place first. That will hold the fringe in the correct position for sewing, and the glue should be hidden. After gluing the fringe into place, allow ample drying time before sewing it to the bow case and quiver.

Once the fringe is sewed into place, fold the quiver over to where the edges meet. By using simple clothespins, clamp the quiver together every two to three inches. That will help you to sew straight and hold the quiver in position. The sewing should be done with the smooth side or fringed side out.

Now start at the bottom and sew to the top with a whipstitch, spacing your stitches evenly and neat. Remove the clothespins as you go. Take a piece of leftover buckskin and cut a circular or oblong piece for the bottom of the quiver. Turn the quiver inside out to sew the bottom piece into place. For extra reinforcement, cut two identical pieces and glue them together, forming a nice thick bottom that metal arrowpoints cannot penetrate. With the bottom sewed into place, turn the quiver back the right way and start on the bow case.

The bow case should be sewed in the same manner as the quiver. When the two pieces are completed, sew the two strap pieces together using the same whipstitch method. A stiffening rod needs to be inserted into the quiver. The rod can protrude from the quiver and be decorated or it can be shorter than the quiver and unseen. The decision is up to the maker.

The rod can be held in place with buckskin thongs cut from the scrap leather. With an awl, make four sets of holes evenly spaced down the quiver. Two of those are going to be used to attach the strap and bow case to the quiver, so place them in a good position.

One hole needs to be toward the top, several inches down from the mouth of the quiver, and one hole several inches up from the bottom. The two in the middle need to be wide enough so that when you attach the strap, the quiver balances well. If the holes are too close together, the quiver will not hang correctly across your back but will tend to lean one way or another.

Loosely thread the buckskin thongs that are going to be used in the top and bottom set of holes through the quiver where the ends are protruding from the back of the quiver. Mark two sets of holes in your bow case to line up with the two middle sets of holes in the quiver. Thread the two buckskin thongs through the holes of the bow case from the back where the ends protrude toward the front. Now thread the same buckskin thongs through the middle sets of holes on the quiver where they protrude from the front.

Once all four are in place, insert the stick down the inside of the quiver so that it goes between the top of the quiver and the buckskin thongs. Next pull the top and bottom thongs tight and secure them with a square knot. When the strap is marked where you want to attach it to the quiver, use the awl to mark a set of holes in each strap. Attach the strap to the remaining set of buckskin thongs and tie them off. The end result is a nice Plains Indian–style quiver.

At this point, if you like, another accessory you might try to make is a small pouch that was often seen on Plains quivers. Called a Strike a Light bag, the pouch was made from stiff leather and contained a flint and steel for fire making, a hide glue stick, pieces of sinew, and maybe a few arrowpoints for repairs in the field. The bags were made in a variety of sizes, but a good average would be four inches wide at the top, seven inches long, and five inches wide at the bottom. Many of them were decorated with tin cones, fringe, beadwork, and German silver. Women wore a similar type of pouch on their belts, normally accompanied by an awl case and knife with sheath.

The Warrior's Tools

When it comes to your quiver, it can remain as it is or be decorated according to your preference. Many good books detail beadwork and quillwork designs favored by the Plains tribes, and beads are readily available at craft stores or online. A good size of seed bead to use in beading is an 11/0 or a 10/0. The 10/0 is slightly larger.

To get started, you will need accompanying needles for the size beads you buy, nylon beading thread, a chunk of beeswax, and a pair of scissors. The most common bead style used by the Plains tribes was called *lazy stitch*.

I have found that sometimes it is easier to do beadwork on separate pieces of buckskin and then attach them to the quiver. If you are an accomplished beadworker already, you can sew right onto the quiver itself.

Chapter 11
Plains Indian Shields

SHIELDS PLAYED AN IMPORTANT role in Plains Indian culture and were often used along with the bow. A warrior on horseback often wore his shield across his back to protect him from incoming arrows. On the ground, the shield could be worn on the bow arm or slid to the side of the body to protect the warrior as he shot arrows.

Most shields were made from the thick hump of an older buffalo bull because the hide was thicker and harder.

Harvested pieces were scraped clean of any flesh and allowed to dry. The dry rawhide disk was then heated and pounded with smooth stones to make it even thicker and harder. The edges of the disk were also pounded on the entire circumference to thicken the edges.

Heat was used to give the shield its dome, whether flat or concave in shape. A shield treated in such a manner could easily stop an arrow or a musket ball.

For some shields, two identical pieces of rawhide were cut and laced together with rawhide or buckskin thongs to make an extremely thick shield.

Interestingly, I have never seen an authentic war shield stretched around a wooden hoop as you see so often today. True war shields were usually made from buffalo rawhide.

The shield was normally comprised of two parts—the shield itself and a cover made from buckskin.

The cover fit around the front of the shield and draped over the back for several inches all the way around. The cover had slits cut at short intervals around the outer edge, and a buckskin thong was laced through the slits, pulled tight, and then tied at the bottom to secure the cover in place.

The inner shield was usually decorated with meaningful symbols, paint, animal effigies, bird feathers, or animal parts, including bear claws, buffalo dewclaws, raptor talons, or the decorative parts of any of a variety of animal that had meaning to the owner. The cover concealed the inner shield, thus protecting the powerful medicine that was on it. *Medicine* here refers to supernatural powers.

A man's shield was always hung in the lodge in the place of honor directly in the back above where the owner sat. Normally, it hung from one the lodgepoles or from cordage draped between the lodgepoles. During the day, the shield was often hung outside on a tripod frame, positioned to directly face the sun, and was rotated throughout the day. It was believed that allowed the shield to soak up the power of the sun.

Taboos were often associated with a shield by which the owner had to strictly abide.

Women were never allowed to touch a war shield. When a woman was on her menstrual cycle, she stayed in another lodge until her cycle was over. Men usually considered a woman's cycle to be powerful medicine and would not want the shield to be in contact with such medicine.

The owner could decorate or paint a shield. Sometimes when a man wanted a shield, he would talk to a holy man, or medicine man, who would then send him to a sweat lodge for purification. The holy man would then instruct the man on something he must do to obtain the right medicine for a shield. Fasting was frequently part of the ritual as the man secluded himself and hoped for a vision. The ritual sometimes included singing, staring at the sun for days at a time, or seeking out certain animals to ask for their power.

If the man seeking his medicine was successful and was graced with an experience, the story would be relayed to the medicine man, who would interpret it and then apply the necessary designs to the shield, according to the story.

Many shields were passed down or inherited by family members. If the shield was taken, all the responsibilities of owning it went with it. Any taboos or rituals had to be strictly followed by the new owner.

Shields were highly respected by the Plains tribes and were believed to not only physically protect the owner but also provide the supernatural powers the shield contained. When the rifle was invented and came on the scene, a bullet fired from one could penetrate a shield with ease. Although that was soon discovered, warriors still carried their shields into battle for their supernatural protecting powers.

Shield covers were decorated differently from the shield itself. Covers were rarely removed from the shield unless exceptional circumstances were at hand. A shield had two buckskin straps on the back to allow the user to slide his arm through when using it. A larger, longer strap allowed the owner to hang the shield over his shoulder when carrying it.

Eric Smith

I have had the privilege of examining two old Plains shields that were documented as having been in battle. The first had no cover but was decorated with tattered feathers that had deteriorated with age. It also carried a human scalp and was painted beautifully with red and black imagery. A large part of the upper middle area of the shield was missing, and several small round holes were around the missing piece. The area around the missing part had originally been painted a brilliant dark red but was splattered with black marks. The damage to the shield was from a point-blank shot from a black-powder shotgun. The old shield and a twelve-foot-long lance had been removed from the fallen warrior who had carried them. Out of respect, I did not touch the shield.

The second shield I examined still had the cover on it and was ochred a mustard yellow color. The only decorations on it were several mescal beans tied to buckskin thongs that hung from the cover. It had an overall dome shape. Although the shield was in good condition, I did not remove the cover, therefore leaving the owner's medicine protected. I have often wondered what the shield itself looked like, but out of respect, I will never know.

I have made several shields for people over the years, but you should know that it is something that has to be done with great respect. I always try to keep in mind that a shield is something special and thus should be handled respectfully.

My own shield took many months to complete. I sought out the right materials and harvested my paint pigments from nature—the way it was done long ago. Nowadays you can buy ochre in many colors. When applying them to a shield, you can mix them with a little water or hide glue to obtain a nice authentic look.

It is not so easy to find good thick buffalo rawhide these days, because buffalo owners tend to keep their old bulls for breeding or for trophy hunters who will pay big bucks to shoot one. What is left comes from younger animals that do not have hide as thick as what the Plains Indians would have used. I have found, however, that buffalo rawhide is readily available. By using some of the same methods, you can make a nice thick shield that will repel an arrow, although I hope nobody will be shooting arrows at you anytime soon!

When it comes to recreating items from the past, you want to be as authentic as possible. In my opinion, you should never copy a historic shield design exactly like the original. Come up with a nice design on your own instead. The possibilities are endless, and then the shield is truly yours.

If you decide to make a shield, there are several tools which will come in handy: gloves, heat gun, awl, heavy rawhide or rubber mallet, and claw hammer. A flat piece of wood large enough to cover the shield will also be needed. Plywood works well for that.

The rawhide disk should be at least twenty inches in diameter—twenty-two inches is even better. If you cannot find buffalo rawhide, you can use elk. I would suggest cutting out two pieces to lace together for a piece thick enough to represent a traditional shield. Historic examples of some shields are those composed of two pieces of rawhide laced together with pages from a book stuffed between the two layers, giving the shield additional thickness.

Once the shield rawhide is in hand, I usually submerge it in hot water for an hour or so until it gets flexible. The rawhide will soak up the water. After only an hour, you should see that the rawhide has become thicker. I allow it to dry for a day or just long enough that it is barely damp to the touch and not pliable any longer. I then use a heat gun to apply heat to the rawhide until most of the moisture is removed. If you are doing this process right, the rawhide will start to curl and become misshapen.

After you get the rawhide extremely hot, lay it on a flat surface—a garage floor works well—and put a piece of lumber on top of it with as much additional weight as is required to force the shield flat. Be sure to wear your gloves while doing that so you don't burn your hands. The weight will force the shield rawhide back to a somewhat flat shape. The shield disk must be left in place until it cools. I normally let it set overnight before I try to remove the board.

When you uncover the rawhide, it will have shrunk in size considerably and will be much harder than before. With a rubber or rawhide mallet, literally beat the shield until every inch of the front and back surface has received a thorough pounding. Next, take the claw hammer and pound the end of the shield until you have gone all the way around it. As you do this, you will notice the edge getting thicker as you go.

If authenticity is important to you, now is the time to test your shield's strength. I like to set my shield up in front of my archery target, get my sinew-backed short bow and a dogwood arrow with an iron trade point, and step back fifteen yards. Then I shoot the disk with the arrow and see what happens.

Of all the shields I have made using this method, I have had only one arrow penetrate a rawhide shield disc. However, even in that instance, the point only went in less than a fourth of an inch and the shaft broke on impact. All of my other shields have survived direct hits from Plains Indian-style arrows from a fifty-pound bow, with the shield either bending the arrowpoint sideways or actually breaking it. I know there is no need to take authenticity that far, but I always like to know if a shield I make would actually stop an arrow if the need arose.

If you use the arrow test and the shield proves impervious, it is ready to be prepped for decoration. Using sandpaper, I sand the edges of my shield and any pieces that might be rough from the preparation process. At that point, you need to decide where your arm straps are going to be placed. Mark two holes for the top of each strap and two holes for the bottom of each strap on one side of the shield. You should also mark where your carrying strap will be. I have found that the carrying strap should be above center and evenly spaced toward the middle of the shield.

I make each set of strap holes one inch apart. Heat the tip of the awl with the heat gun or over the stove and bore the strap holes into the shield. It will be necessary to reheat the awl several times.

After you have made the holes, the shield is ready to be painted. Ochre is best to paint shields because it gives an authentic look; modern paints are too vibrant and thick in my opinion.

Watercolors are a good substitute for ochre but they tend to rub off if not mixed with hide glue. Yellow, blue, black, rust red, red, and green are good colors for shields. Ochre can be mixed with a small amount of water or hide glue and applied with a paintbrush, your fingers, a wooden dowel sharpened on the end, or even a Q-tip.

Draw out your design with a pencil beforehand, and then paint your shield accordingly. After the shield is dry, you can give it an aged appearance by roughing up the surface here and there with sandpaper. Or if you prefer, you can take a handful of dry dirt and thoroughly rub it into the shield, somewhat fading the colors.

You can add any decorations you want to personalize the shield. You can buy hand-painted reproductions of most raptor feathers online. A set of imitation golden eagle tail feathers will really stand out. You can bind the feathers at the quill with cloth of various colors and beaded or wrapped with buckskin. You can also make small medicine bags of buckskin to tie to the shield. Brass or copper hawkbells, thimbles, ermine skins, foxtails, buffalo or horse tails, and any number of legal animal parts can be incorporated to give the shield a unique look. I would suggest looking at historical examples for inspiration in your decorations—you don't want to overdo it.

With your shield decorated, you can attach the carrying strap and arm straps with buckskin thongs, and then leave the shield as it is or construct a shield cover. I know of only a few people who not only make Plains Indians shields in the traditional manner using buffalo rawhide but also take the time to make the cover for the shield, despite the fact that a shield without a cover looks unfinished, in my opinion.

You can always display the shield and cover as two separate pieces hanging side by side on the wall. A simple piece of thick cardboard cut to the same dimension of the shield can be inserted into your cover if you want to show its shape and purpose. When hung next to the shield, it makes for a stunning display.

When you make the cover for the shield, you will need a hide big enough for the job. Again, I use smoked brain-tanned buckskin for this and find there is absolutely no substitute. However, you might also consider what is called German-tanned buckskin if you cannot find brain-tanned hide.

German-tanned buckskin comes from the European red stag, and it has a texture similar to brain-tanned hide. It is even smoked, giving the hide a nice rich color. A ten-foot-square hide is more than enough for a shield and should give you enough extra for the carrying strap and arm straps if you don't have any buckskin for those pieces.

I always lay my shield in the center of the hide and draw a circle three inches wider around than the shield itself. The extra three inches will be the part of the cover that fits over onto the back of the shield. Draw out your line with a pencil before cutting to avoid making an error.

After the piece of buckskin is cut out, cut slits three-quarter-of-inch long spaced one inch apart all the way around the edge approximately an inch from the outer edge. Then cut a buckskin thong a half-inch thick but long enough to go all around the cover.

Lace the buckskin thong in and out of the holes until the two ends meet. Lay your shield facedown on the cover and fold the edges over it. If you have feathers attached to the shield, fold them and any other decorations that might hang from the shield up under it so they do not hang out around the edges. As you tighten the buckskin thong, the cover will cinch up around the shield. Make sure you have adjusted the cover evenly around the shield before tying the two ends at the bottom.

After the cover is adjusted to your liking, you can paint it on the shield or you can remove it from the shield for decorating. I usually remove the cover and decorate it before reattaching it to the shield.

The cover can be painted in the same manner as the shield, but you will not need to use hide glue. The buckskin will soak up the ochre or watercolor. It will not run unless the cover is soaking wet.

I enjoy painting the cover of a shield more than I do the shield itself because the pigment soaks into the buckskin well, and I can do more detailed line work.

I seldom draw out my design on the cover, preferring to work from previously made sketches of my chosen design. The last shield cover I made showed two grizzly bears facing each other with open mouths and oversized claws. It was a nice design that also had several other elements on the outer edge of the cover.

If needed, you could draw your designs on the hide with a pencil, but I will warn you that if you mess up, it is hard to get the pencil lines out of the hide. Take your time instead and draw your designs ever so lightly on the hide. If you mess up, you can gently sand the pencil line with sandpaper, removing the line to some degree, depending on how lightly it was drawn.

After you paint the cover, you can decorate it in a manner that is pleasing to you, using the same techniques you incorporated into the shield.

Eric Smith

Your imagination is the only limit on what you can create. With such a vast array of historical shield images available, you can create a piece that will make you proud.

Chapter 12
Final Thoughts

AS THIS WRITING IS ENDING, I hope your bow-making adventures will begin and you can apply some of what you learned here to practical use. Remember that I wrote from a Native American bowyer's perspective. That being said, I tried to provide modern ways to achieve some of the same traditional results. If these writings inspire just one of my readers to get out and work on any of the historical pieces in this book, then I will feel my efforts were worthy.

You will always have failures and defeats in your bow making, but I promise that you will gain valuable experience with each one just as you will with each success.

It is hard to learn to make a bow from one book, and many books have been written on the subject. It is my hope that this book brings doable methods and a new commonsense perspective that is easy to read and understand. I have discussed my modern methods while describing traditional methods used by the Plains

Indians, and in the end, as we found, there are only a few differences.

Everything is debatable when it comes to recreating the past, but common sense and thirty years of bow building have taught me many things about Plains Indian archery. First and foremost, there is no easy way to make a traditional bow. Instead, we have a few principles that need to be followed to get the desired end result. I am certain that the more you practice, the better you will become at it.

It takes years to learn wood because all wood is different. Even wood of the same species and cut from the same area can have different characteristics. It will take some trial and error for you to figure out what you want to use for bowwood and what woods are best set aside. Even a seasoned bowyer can get frustrated by the process at times. When you get to that point, it is best to set your project aside and take a break.

Many times during the years, when I was working on a bow-related project, I have had the proverbial light bulb flash above my head and had a bow-making revelation. I found a way of doing something better than I had been doing it previously.

When I show bows I have made to the youngsters in my classes, they always want to make a recurved bow or a reflexed bow or a sinew-backed bow like some of the ones I've shown. I show them those bows so they can see what they could create with some practice, but they need to walk before they can run. Until you have ten good self bows under your belt, I would not try to make bows of other designs.

If there is anything I can't stress enough when it comes to increasing your odds of bow-making success, it is to use quality materials and to practice. Learn the basics first, and then experiment with other designs after you have completed a few good D-shaped self bows.

The Warrior's Tools

There are several woods that are tough, durable, and easy to work with, and they will also help your odds. Two that I would suggest are Osage orange, or bois d'arc, and hickory. Hickory will be a little more forgiving than Osage orange because it can withstand more growth-ring violation than any other wood and still make a good working bow. Osage is a better wood, in my opinion, but it will be more expensive than a hickory stave of similar size.

Basic essential tools include a drawknife, a wood rasp, a chainsaw file, a pocketknife, and various grits of sandpaper. All of those should cost less than a hundred dollars total. As you progress in your bow making, you can add more tools if you like.

One thing is for certain: I can promise you there are few feelings more rewarding than making a fine bow for the first time. I have forgotten about so many bows I have made over the decades, but I will always remember my first one.

I also still remember the first animal that I harvested with a homemade bow and arrow, every detail of the hunt—drawing the bow, watching the arrow as if in slow motion arch toward the animal, and then seeing the feathers disappear into the rib cage. The feeling of accomplishment and the connection with our ancestors that followed is indescribable.

In conclusion, there are no deep, dark, hidden secrets to making the Plains Indian bow and arrow.

You just need the materials, the tools, and the patience.

Glossary

anchor point: A known point on the body or face to be touched by the drawing hand when the bow is ready to shoot.

archer: A person who practices archery.

archer's paradox: The effect of an arrow as it bends around the handle of the bow when released.

arm guard, bracer: A protective piece of material worn on the forearm to protect the arm and wrist from the bowstring.

arrow: The projectile shot from a bow.

Anatomy of a Plains Indian Arrow

Arrow

arrowhead, arrowpoint: The front end of an arrow, also known as the head, point, or tip.

back: The side of the bow that holds tension and faces away from the archer when bow is held in hand in the shooting position.

bark: The outermost layer on the bowstave.

belly: The compression side of the bow that faces the archer when the bow is held in the hand ready to shoot.

bow: A tool or weapon used to propel an arrow made of a strip of flexible material, such as wood, with a cord connecting the two ends that holds the wood strip bent.

bow case: A pouch in which an unbraced bow is carried.

bowstave, stave: A strip or rod of wood cut from a larger piece of wood, trimmed, and intended to be made into a bow.

bowstring: A fibrous material joining two ends of an archer's bow, comprised of multiple strands of material twisted to form a bowstring. Strings can be made of various materials, including linen, flax, sinew, and Dacron B-50.

bowyer, bow maker, bowman: A person who makes bows.

brace, braced: The act of attaching a bowstring to a bow.

brace height: The distance between the string and the bow's handle when the bow is braced.

The Warrior's Tools

Plains Indian Bow

"D" Bow

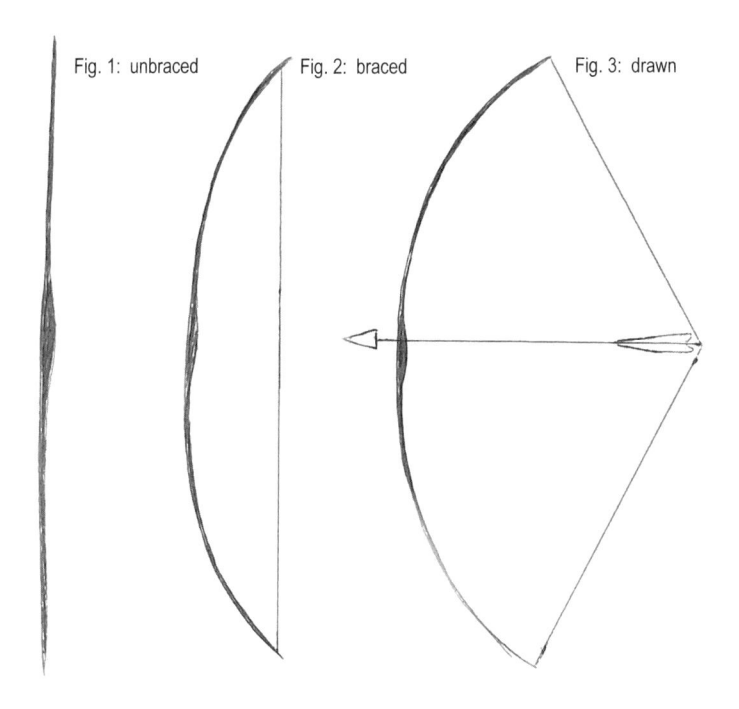

Fig. 1: unbraced

Fig. 2: braced

Fig. 3: drawn

braced bow: A bow that has the string affixed to the nocks and is secured taut making the bow ready to be drawn.

butcher knife: A large single-edged kitchen knife preferred by butchers for its durability and heavy feel. The wide blade is smooth, without serrated edges, and curves up at the end.

chainsaw file: A small round file used mainly to sharpen chainsaw blades but also the ideal size to make nocks in the ends of a bow.

cock feather, index feather: A feather that indicates proper arrow alignment on the string.

composite bow: A bow made from more than one natural material, such as sinew, horn, or wood.

deflex bow: A bow in which the entire length or part of the limbs curve toward the archer.

draw, drawing: The act of pulling back the bowstring that is attached to the bow.

drawknife: A knife with a handle at each end of a straight or slightly curved blade, used mainly in a pulling motion toward the user. The handles are placed at right angles. The blade has a flat edge on the bottom and a sharp edge on top.

draw length: Distance a bow is or can be drawn by the archer.

draw weight: The number of pounds of force required to draw a bow. Draw weight is measured at the bow's maximum draw length.

five-curve bow: A bow with five total curves throughout the handle and limbs.

fletching: The stabilizing feathers attached to an arrow.

The Warrior's Tools

Plains Indian Bow Styles

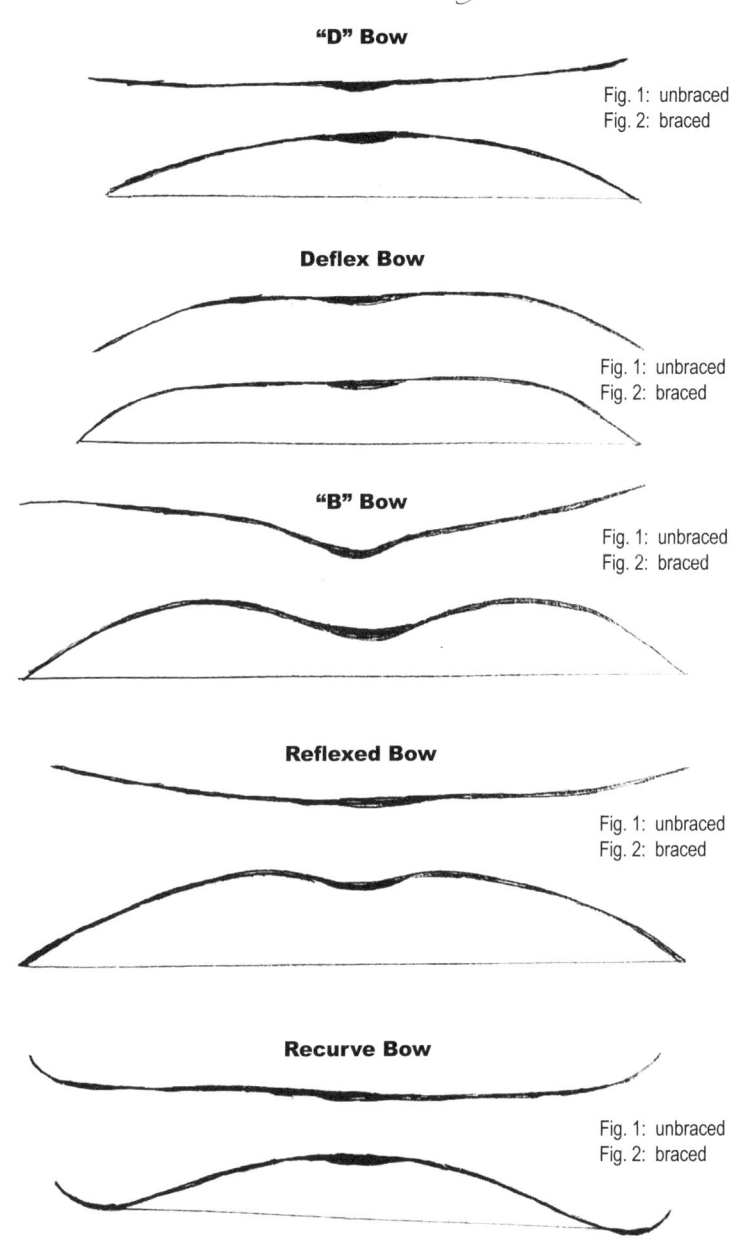

"D" Bow

Fig. 1: unbraced
Fig. 2: braced

Deflex Bow

Fig. 1: unbraced
Fig. 2: braced

"B" Bow

Fig. 1: unbraced
Fig. 2: braced

Reflexed Bow

Fig. 1: unbraced
Fig. 2: braced

Recurve Bow

Fig. 1: unbraced
Fig. 2: braced

growth ring: A layer of wood produced during a single period of growth. As the tree grows, more layers are developed, each adding a ring if looked at as a cross section of the tree. The outermost layers are the newest.

handle, grip: The section where the bow is held when shooting.

hardwood, heartwood: The layer of wood under the sapwood that is layered to construct the back of the bow.

hinge: A sharp angle in a spot on a bow, indicating a spot that has been overworked. A hinge in a bow usually requires the bow to be discarded.

horse archer: An archer mounted on a horse.

loose: The act of shooting an arrow from a bow.

midlimb: The middle section of a bow's upper and lower limbs.

nock: The notch that has been cut at the end of an arrow; also, the notches at the ends of the bow limbs to which the bowstring is attached or looped over.

nocking: The act of setting an arrow on a bowstring.

nocking point: The point on a bowstring where the arrow nock is placed.

overdraw: A condition in which a bow is drawn past or over its expected draw length.

Plains Indians or Indigenous people of the Great Plains and Canadian Prairies: Native American tribes and First Nation band governments who have traditionally lived on the greater Interior Plains (i.e. the Great Plains and the Canadian Prairies) in North America. Their historic nomadic culture and development of equestrian culture and resistance to domination by the government and military forces of Canada and the United States made the Plains Indian culture groups an archetype in literature and art for American Indians everywhere, and many of the tribes continue to thrive and influence the regions in which they are based to this day.

point: The front end of an arrow, also known as the arrowhead, head, or tip.

quiver: A pouch or case in which an archer's arrows are carried or stored.

rasp: A coarse file, usually a hand tool, with sharp, pointed projections on each of two flat sides, used for shaping wood. In most cases, one side is rougher than the other.

recurve bow: A bow in which tips curve away from the archer.

reflex bow: A bow in which the entire length of the handle and limbs curve away from the archer.

release: The act of shooting an arrow from a bow.

sapwood: The soft outer layers of recently formed wood found directly under the bark, between the heartwood and the bark.

self bow: A bow made all of wood, usually from a single piece.

shaft: The main structural element of an arrow.

spine: The stiffness of an arrow shaft or how much flex an arrow has throughout its length.

stacking: The action in which a bow gains draw weight rapidly the last few inches of draw.

stave: A strip of wood, usually split from a larger piece, intended for making a bow.

Strike a Light bag: A pouch made from stiff leather; used by Plains bowyers to hold flint and steel for fire making, as well as a hide glue stick, pieces of sinew, and maybe a few arrowpoints for repairs in the field.

tiller: The action that causes the bow to bend the same on the upper and lower limbs causing a pleasing arch of the bow.

tillering stick: A piece of wood usually three feet in length with a "U" shape cut in the end and rows of notches cut at one-inch intervals. The handle of the bow fits into the U-shaped notch, and the string is drawn down to one of the grooves, putting the bow in a drawn state. Used to help a bow maker see where the bow needs to be tillered. As bow is tillered to shape, the bow maker can pull the string farther on the stick, checking the tiller at various draw lengths until the ideal tiller is achieved at the draw length the archer desires.

tip, tips: The two end points of the bow; the end of an arrow.

unbraced bow: A bow that does not have the string affixed to the nocks.

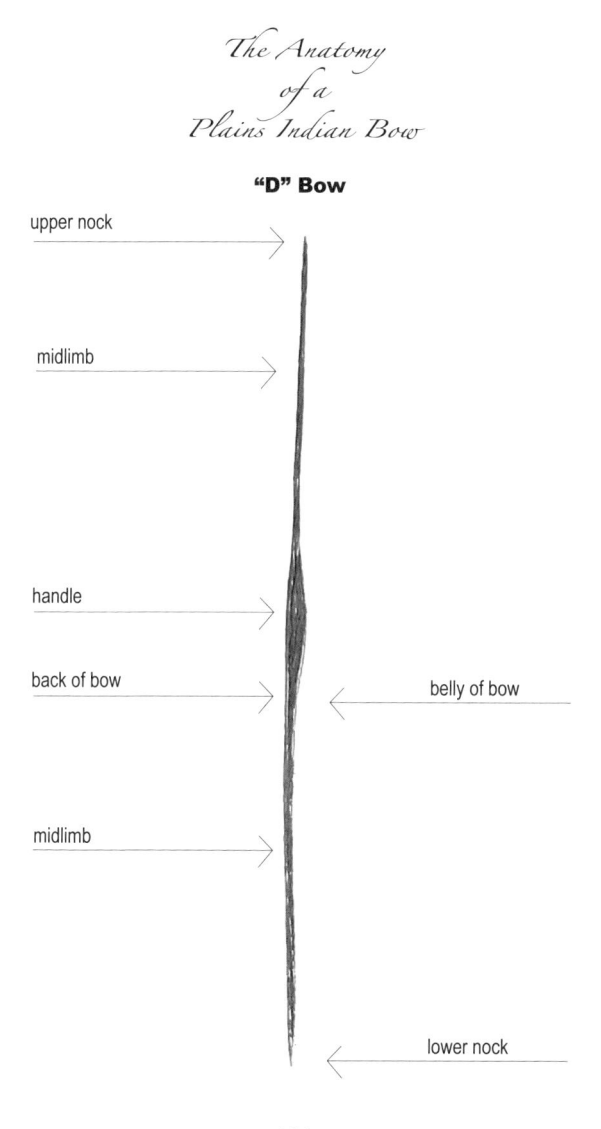

The Anatomy of a Plains Indian Bow

"D" Bow

- upper nock
- midlimb
- handle
- back of bow
- belly of bow
- midlimb
- lower nock

About the Author

Chickasaw author Eric Smith is a master bowyer who has taught the ancient craft of bow making to Native American youth and others across the country—his creations have appeared in Hollywood movies, including *The Revenant*, and grace museums and collections in more than twenty-six countries. He makes his home in central Oklahoma.

Acknowledgments

I would like to give special thanks to The RoadRunner Press, Dr. Kent Smith, Towana Spivey, Donna Richards, and Sandra LeBeau for their help in bringing this book to fruition.